# The Dramaturgy of Space

OTHER TITLES IN THE THEATRE MAKERS SERIES:

*The Art of Resonance* by Anne Bogart

*Adrian Lester and Lolita Chakrabarti: A Working Diary*
by Adrian Lester and Lolita Chakrabarti

*The Uncapturable* by Rubén Szuchmacher, translated
by William Gregory

*Julie Hesmondhalgh: A Working Diary* by Julie Hesmondhalgh

*Julius Caesar and Me: Exploring Shakespeare's African Play*
by Paterson Joseph

*Simon Stephens: A Working Diary* by Simon Stephens

*Devising Theatre with Stan's Cafe*
by Mark Crossley and James Yarker

*Meyerhold on Theatre* by Edward Braum

*Edward Bond: The Playwright Speaks*
by David Tuaillon with Edward Bond

*Joan's Book: The Autobiography of Joan Littlewood*
by Joan Littlewood, introduced by Philip Hedley

*Steppenwolf Theatre Company of Chicago* by John Mayer

# The Dramaturgy of Space

*Ramón Griffero*
*Translated by Adam Versényi*

methuen | drama
LONDON • NEW YORK • OXFORD • NEW DELHI • SYDNEY

METHUEN DRAMA
Bloomsbury Publishing Plc
50 Bedford Square, London, WC1B 3DP, UK
1385 Broadway, New York, NY 10018, USA
29 Earlsfort Terrace, Dublin 2, Ireland

BLOOMSBURY, METHUEN DRAMA and the Methuen Drama logo are trademarks of Bloomsbury Publishing Plc

First published in Chile as *La Dramaturgia del Espacio* by Ediciones Frontera Sur 2011
This edition published by Methuen Drama 2022

Copyright © Ramón Griffero, 2011, 2022
Translation copyright © Adam Versényi, 2022

Ramón Griffero has asserted his right under the Copyright, Designs and Patents Act, 1988, to be identified as author of this work.

For legal purposes the Acknowledgments on pp. xii–xiii constitute an extension of this copyright page.

Cover design: Ben Anslow
Cover image © Cárlos Cohl Griffero

All rights reserved. No part of this publication may be reproduced or transmitted in any form or by any means, electronic or mechanical, including photocopying, recording, or any information storage or retrieval system, without prior permission in writing from the publishers.

Bloomsbury Publishing Plc does not have any control over, or responsibility for, any third-party websites referred to or in this book. All internet addresses given in this book were correct at the time of going to press. The author and publisher regret any inconvenience caused if addresses have changed or sites have ceased to exist, but can accept no responsibility for any such changes.

A catalogue record for this book is available from the British Library.

A catalog record for this book is available from the Library of Congress.

| ISBN: | HB: | 978-1-3502-3558-8 |
|---|---|---|
| | PB: | 978-1-3502-3559-5 |
| | ePDF: | 978-1-3502-3560-1 |
| | eBook: | 978-1-3502-3561-8 |

Series: Theatre Makers

Typeset by Integra Software Services Pvt. Ltd.
Printed and bound in Great Britain

To find out more about our authors and books visit www.bloomsbury.com and sign up for our newsletters.

# CONTENTS

*Preface* viii
*Acknowledgments* xii

## CHAPTER I 1
A Beginning 1
The Dramaturgy of Space—Its Origin 2
Art and Existence 5
Atavism and Art 9
Gestures of Expression or of Creation 13
Virtuosity and Authorship in the Gesture of Creation 15
Speaking from a Place: The Relationship between the Center and the Periphery 16
Art and Politics 19
Earlier Scenic Models and Original Authorship 24
Decontextualization as the Premise for a Fiction's Perception 30
The Scenic Space and its Support 33
The Rectangle as Format in the Age of Social Rectangularization 34
Of the Circular 36
History of Art and Rectangular Composition 37
The Stage Space and the Theatre Building 38

## CHAPTER II 43
Approaches to The Dramaturgy of Space 43
The Dissection of the Format 45

Body and Decontextualization of the Stage Space 47
The Organic Composition (Functional and Intimate) 50
Points of Focus in the Stage Space 53
The Use of Focus for Organization in Large Spaces, and with Big Groups 55
Typology of Focal Points in the Stage Space 55
Focal Points: Composition and Content 60
Graphic Corporeal Composition 61
Organic-Graphic Composition and Costuming 62
The Body and Geometric Narrative of the Format 64
Symmetry and Asymmetry 68
Symmetry—Asymmetry in Corporeal Composition 69
Of the Actorly Body in the Space: The Poetics of the Body 72
A Story Passes through the Story of the Body–Space it Represents 75
The Dramaturgy of the Object 77
The Decontextualization of the Object 79
The Spatial Narrtive of the Object 80
Body and Object 81
Body and Object in Functional Relationship 83
Plastic Object-Body Dramaturgy 84
Body-Object and Geometry 86
The Object in its Metaphorical Function 88
The Absurd Object 88
Object Nomenclature to Consider in the Exercises 89
The Dramaturgy of the Conceptual Object 90
Objects of Scenic Artifice as Concepts 98
Animals in the Dramaturgy of Space 99
Conceptual Acting 100
Actorial Body and Appropriation of a Place of Fiction 102
The Fictional Place as Concept 107
Cinematification of the Stage 109
Theatricalization of Film 109
The Planes of the Body and Spatial Temporal Dimensions 111

## CHAPTER III  119
Relationships between a Poetics of Space and
  the Poetics of a Text  119
The Dramatic Text as a Construction in Process  119
The Impossibility of Speaking Like Writing  124
Our Emotions Are Mute: The Theatre Gives Them Voice  125
What is Named Exists, or, the Empowerment of
  Knowledge  126
Writing and Social Linguistic Structures  127
The Tradition of Dramatic Language as Reference for
  Contemporary Writings  128
Of the Appropriation of a Text  129

## CHAPTER IV  133
Dramaturgy of Space in Scenic Practice  133
Poetics of Text and Space/Place  134
Visual Productions of the Poetics of Abstract Space  148
Textual Poetics—Conceptual Spaces  154

*Epilogue*  171

# PREFACE

*Religion creates rites based in dogmas. Theatre generates rites for transformation.*
– RAMÓN GRIFFERO, THE DRAMATURGY OF SPACE

The Dramaturgy of Space, first published in Chile in 2011 and updated by Griffero for this English edition in 2021, describes Griffero's aesthetic philosophy, his theoretical approach to theatrical creation, and illustrates that theory through practical application in a series of exercises. For much too long Western European/North American scholars and practitioners have theorized about Latin American theatre, imposing their own interpretations upon theatrical creation throughout the region, while the voices of Latin American practitioners themselves have barely been heard. The most prominent exception to this is Agosto Boal's work (and, to a lesser extent, that of Enrique Buenaventura, Alejandro Jodorowsky, and Rubén Szchumacher), but much of Boal's career was spent outside of Latin America. While the 1973 military coup against the democratically elected government of Salvador Allende forced Ramón Griffero into exile where he completed undergraduate work in Sociology in England, and graduate work in theatre in Belgium, he returned to Chile in the early 1980s, founded the theatre company Teatro de Fin de Siglo, and opened El Trolley, a cultural space for resistance to the Pinochet dictatorship. Situated in an unfashionable part of town "between a brothel and a prison," El Trolley's productions were funded by parties, gigs, and art events attended by a largely young audience in search of a range of political and artistic responses to the complex realities of living under a repressive regime. What Griffero describes as El Trolley's "pre-capitalist marginality" constituted its freedom, the site from which he established his political poetics and his dramaturgy of space.

From its inception, Griffero's work in Chile, forcefully stated in his 1985 "Manifesto for an Autonomous Theatre," sought artistic, political, and aesthetic alternatives to the language of the dictatorship. Rejecting prevalent artistic and aesthetic forms, Teatro de Fin de Siglo experimented with creative ways of seeing what appears onstage, consciously developing a political way of viewing the stage and honing a politics of art capable of transgressing, subverting, and transforming the theatrical language then in vogue. *The Dramaturgy of Space* is simultaneously a memoir of one of the most influential artists contributing to the renovation of the Chilean theatre in the 1980s and 1990s, and a platform from which Griffero has launched his creative work up until the present day.

In her review of Griffero's book *The Dramaturgy of Space*, Vivian Martínez Tabares writes that the book

> summarizes an attitude towards theatrical creation that defends its autonomy, reconstitutes human existential notions such as death, the universe, desires or happiness and projects social fictions that allow us to imagine other sociopolitical orders; the assumption that space must take on the rectangular format—the option chosen by the West to project all our thoughts—is replaced by circular perception that sees the stage as a creative space that allows the recontextualization of language in order to create a visual narrative that abstracts the sign of representation (text, body, music, objects) in order to introduce them in the scenic space and generate fictions within the rectangular space … In the midst of the Pinochet dictatorship, the stage became a territory in which human imagination generated non-existent fictions within which our world could be reconstructed, deconstructed, and reformulated.
>
> (Vivian Martínez Tabares, "Vida, performance y política en *La dramaturgia del espacio*," Revista *Conjunto*, Casas de las Americas)

After noting in *The Dramaturgy of Space* that, despite the fact that we live on a circular planet illuminated by stars of the same form, blackboards, houses, windows, TV and computer screens, flags, beds, and coffins are all rectangular, the author asks:

When and how did we become separated from our circular condition? Was it when we broke our organic union with nature? Was it when the human being, in his evolution, stopped perceiving or feeling like the animals that we primarily are? Is it the product of civilization, a psychic change, where the axis of our relationship to the cosmos and nature—where rectangular forms are absent—is displaced and internalized apart from our own physiological construction?

On one level Griffero's conception of a "dramaturgy of space" is a rearticulation in Chilean terms of European avant-garde artists such as Adolphe Appia, Edward Gordon Craig, Jean Cocteau, and Antonin Artaud, each of whom in their own way called for theatre of the theatre itself, a kind of creation that could only appear on the stage. As Griffero has stated,

> The body, the gesture, sounds, music, light, objects, scenic elements, constructed places, time, and the use of planes and compositions all intervene in the poetics of space. One reads the space, it generates ideas and emotions. A body in a place, an object on another plane, music, dripping, geese running across the space, etc., etc., all constitute the poetics of space elaborated upon by a text. A theatre without a poetics of space is a literary act represented and a theatre without a textual poetics is a summation of images.
> (Ramón Griffero, "*Almuerzo de mediodía o Brunch*" in *Apuntes* No. 117)

As an example of the dramaturgy of space, what Griffero is describing here is his own reconfiguration of Cocteau's distinction between "poetry *of* the theatre" as distinct from "poetry *in* the theatre," where the latter corresponds to Griffero's contention that too many playwrights merely put literature on the stage, instead of conceiving of a theatricality that can only be created on the stage, that is *of* the theatre. The difference between the European theatrical innovators I have cited and what Griffero is after can be found in Griffero's particularly late-twentieth/early-twenty-first-century Chilean context and its focus on the importance of memory.

As Catherine Boyle has described his work:

> Griffero's dramatic imagination sees all the elements of the production together, to be embodied onstage in a complex accumulation of his language of textual, visual, physical and conceptual signs. In this there is a profound sense of what he calls "scenic memory", a history of the stage that contains all its actors in each dense moment. In a world where an increasing lack or defiance of historical consciousness threatens us all, Ramón Griffero's insistence on the creation of scenic languages that provide the possibility of performing the complex historic multiplicity of our individual and collective being is worth the effort of recreating.
> (Catherine Boyle, "Introduction," *Ramón Griffero: Your Desires in Fragments and Other Plays*, xxi, London: Oberon Books, 2016)

Ultimately, Griffero's work as playwright and director discards a colonial attitude to theatrical creation that accepts the rectangular stage format as the context for creation and, instead, seeks to subvert that predetermined paradigm by focusing upon the stage as an abstract space with its own poetics of space that allow a multiplicity of visual and narrative constructions. The exercises in *The Dramaturgy of Space* are designed to enable practitioners to create their own stage alphabet. By working with the body and object in space, actors, directors, and playwrights can explore how to build their own spatial narratives.

Griffero's plays and productions from the 1980s to the present are essential components in the resurgence of contemporary Chilean theatre. His creative work continues to be prominent in Chile's artistic life. The beauty of *The Dramaturgy of Space* is its combination of theory and practice. Whenever Griffero ventures into the realm of abstract theory he then grounds his ideas in concrete examples from his own productions of his plays, or in practical exercises that illustrate what he seeks to achieve. The politics of *The Dramaturgy of Space* turns to the creative power of the theatre as a site for an ontological rebirth that moves beyond spoken discourse to enable us, like the theatre it describes, to discover and transform ourselves.

# ACKNOWLEDGMENTS

## Author's Acknowledgments

All those who have contributed to this book's elaboration are theatre professionals. In addition to their multiple artistic activities they have been active participants in the academic and creative processes that led to this theoretical reflection's development. I owe them my gratitude.

Research Assistant: Ricardo Balic
Design: Javiera Torres
Musical Composition: Alejandro Miranda
Video: Carlos Cohl
Photographs: Francisco Albornoz
**Actors and Actresses in the Scenic Realizations**
Taira Court
Ximena Rivas
Antonia Zegers
Virginia Beltrami
Claudio Marin
Omar Moran
Mario Horton
Italo Spotorno
Ricardo Balic
Javiera Torres
Intellectual Property Registration No. 208445

## Translator's Acknowledgments

Anna Brewer, Meredith Benson, and the entire team at Methuen Drama have been a joy to work with on this project from beginning to end. I thank them for their grace and professionalism. Early drafts of this translation were written with the assistance of the Eugene O'Neill Foundation's Travis Bogard Artist in Residence Fellowship at Tao House in Danville, California, and the assistance of another writing residency at Seoul Arts Space, Yeonhui, Seoul, South Korea. I am grateful to both organizations for the opportunity to work uninterrupted. Robin Kirk accompanied me in both California and South Korea and kept me grounded as we explored the headlands of Mendocino and hiked the Free State of Jones, or indulged in delicious delicacies in the alleys of Seoul, climbed in the mountains above Busan, and trudged through the muck and mud after elephants in Mondulkiri, Cambodia. As the work on this translation ebbed and flowed, I have watched in wonder as my daughters Elena and Nina have grown into glorious young women. To all three my love.

# CHAPTER I

*Theatre is my life, which is why I never tire of it,
I think its life itself that tires me.*

– HERBERT JONCKERS

## A Beginning

From an apartment in Brussels in 1980 I observed the tiled roofs marching into the distance across the gray, cloudy background of the city while I typed my first play, *Opera pour un Naufrage*. At the time I didn't sense I had started to follow the path I'd keep on until today: shaping texts and images emerging from a cranium to manifest themselves on a stage. Nor could I glimpse that I was beginning to scrutinize the world of representation, and that the confrontation with this necessity to shape subversions, desires, and pleasures would take me places where the doors of creation would break open locks on other doors that, if not hidden, were unknown. Even today I can't say that I've exhausted thresholds to cross, or that one can find the Holy Grail of scenic art where two roads diverge.

Writing challenged forms of representation, texts were interrogated so that bodies spoke, and the stage became the basis of so many laborious studies—visualizations of emotional contents that chose this format in which to manifest themselves. I wrote from exile, for a place somewhere beyond my personal situation. A dialogue of being with art, trying to express an unofficial story.

But we're talking about an art that didn't end in that apartment, that requires interlocutors and others who can visualize and concretize those texts. That's where meetings with those who keep opening places arise.

Meeting Herbert Jonckers[1] gave this first text a spatial narrative, which he began to build in the pantry/wine cellar of that house; to define the concepts, the temporal scenic areas, the objects, the faces to make-up: he began to give it a vision so distinct from the written, that I was confronted with the infinite nature of an artistic language.

Twenty-six years later, I am examining in this book some of the artistic thoughts, actions, creations, and exercises, that have constructed what I am calling The Dramaturgy of Space. Its definition will become clear as it is sketched over the course of the book's chapters.

This is a glance at gestures of creation that give us perspectives on artistic action. In no sense is it meant to establish a model but is presented as a theoretical elaboration of an artistic experience. As such, the book is incapable of encompassing the sum total of that experience's metaphysics, its continuity, or its constant explosion.

The exercises and reflections in this book are directed towards those seeking a space to trigger their own convictions, to generate their own theatrical activity. And towards those who want to see the world of representation from another place. Last, but not least, they register and point out that creative work and theories about an art of the species gestate in other territories of this planet as well.

Let's begin, then, this journey that, for all the linear continuity of its pages, takes us through a horizontal structure, while maintaining the perception that these sentences form part of a universe containing several dimensions that coexist.

# The Dramaturgy of Space—Its Origin

The concept of The Dramaturgy of Space is proposed as a way to think about the theatre that departs from practice with and reflection upon its format: space. A format for the construction of scenic languages and, of course, authorship.

---

[1] Visual artist and designer (integral) (1954–96). He worked with the author on his first productions in Belgium. In 1982 he moved to Chile, spurring fundamental change in the development of contemporary Chilean theatre design. *Poéticas de Espacio Escénico. Herbert Jonckers. Chile 1981–1996*, Santiago de Chile: Ediciones Frontera Sur, 2006.

# CHAPTER I

In my theatrical practice, as much in writing as in production, there are two elaborations that for me have been the axis of scenic creation, that of "Textual Poetics" and its interaction with the "Poetics of Space." These two instances produce a single piece of writing. The scenic fact.

When I had to define the foundations of my relationship with theatre arts, I combined these two terms beneath that of The Dramaturgy of Space. This perception confronts the scenic fact as much in its writing as in its manifestation upon the stage.

Dramatic writing for a spatial format. A spatial construction for dramatic writing.

Here I develop a re-elaboration of what I have received from theatrical tradition, and of what I have received from my Western cultural formation.

But above all, from the contributions that my friend and set designer Herbert Jonckers offered me during sixteen years of work. With his creative obsession in the formulation of spaces, he built forms and designs that transgressed what existed in order to generate the spatial fiction of a text and allow me to see the hidden. There are also the contributions generated during the process of creation with actors, actresses, lighting designers, visual artists, set designers, and the audience.

And essentially, everyone who has been involved with Teatro Fin de Siglo's productions. Finally, we can add the presence of the hundreds of students in courses and workshops on The Dramaturgy of Space that have taken place with professionals in different countries who have made these principles theirs and have given life to the exercises described here.

Viewing the spatial narrative of the scenic fact from another perspective also led to my first addiction to this phenomenon, to making this concept appear, elaborated in such a way as to point out the compositions inside the rectangle that generate stories and their forms.

The need to approach the stage from other perspectives arose out of a political conviction, one that believes in the power of the theatre to construct discourses and languages that are dissident, alternatives to the discourses that want to determine our perception and feelings about our history, our existence, and the facts that surround us and are ours to live.

At the beginning, I postulated in *Manifesto for an Autonomous Theatre*, written in 1985, that the only tool I had to resist the dictatorship was art, in this case the theatre. In that historical context, the principle was: "We have to change the codes and images of the theatrical form so that we don't talk like they talk, so that we don't see like they see, so that we don't show what they show. We have to return to the alphabet, decode the vowels of scenic language first." Naming in this "they" not only the authoritarian gaze, but also "certain artistic and political ways of seeing centered in reiterated languages or pre-existing models."

From there came a self-definition: I will situate myself as dissenting as much from authoritarian power as from official dissent, sliding away from cultural forms or theatrical expressions that had already lost their capacity for transgression or subversion. "Autonomous because nothing they've given us do we owe them, autonomous because we will auto sustain ourselves and auto generate ourselves." Postulating the artistic conception of being dissidents from dissent, and an autonomous art in the face of political discourses that have lost their fictional truth.

The theatre should be a form of subversion, but for that to surge forth it was urgent to change the means of representation which, through use, had lost scenic truth or had returned to the quotidian.

I was convinced by the principles of artistic subversion at the beginning of the twentieth century, where the vanguards postulated a break from preceding models, with creative structures that aspired not only to artistic subversion, but towards the gestation of other social relations. The utopias they wanted to establish needed ad hoc artistic forms, in order to create the culture of the "new man."

Today these aspirations of social intervention seem ingenuous to us; nevertheless, they re-elaborated and enlarged the signs and codes of representation and generated visions of change and a perception of reality departing from the politics of art.

That was why I named our action in 1984 *Teatro de Fin de Siglo*, as an homage to the artistic movements from when the twentieth century was young, and therefore resistant to and rebelling against the inheritance of the nineteenth century. A metaphor for a rebellion that was cruelly repressed by the authoritarian fathers that would emerge and crush these new perceptions. The arrival of Mussolini in 1928, Stalin in 1931, Hitler in 1933, and Franco in 1936 was a violent reaction against other fictions that could constitute themselves in reality. Then, the Second World War and the bipolarity of the Cold War prolonged and justified the necessity for the patriarchal powers in the face of whatever undermined their ways of seeing and governing the planet. If they permitted the end of the colonial period with the collapse of now unmasked colonial empires—English, French, or German—they gave way to the emergence of authoritarian systems, products of colonial revolutions where, amidst traditional, authoritarian, and monarchical regimes, they institutionalized the annulment of creation. All to end in our new era of globalization and uniformity of markets and mentalities so that the new imperial system can continue.

The name *Teatro de Fin de Siglo*, besides being an homage to the artistic creation of the beginning of the twentieth century, was also a challenge to those who constituted it, since it gave us a place and a period in which to realize our proposals: the period between 1983 and 2000, sensing that this was the period during which we should conceive or announce our visions and creations.

So, we resisted the dictatorship in order to sense the democratic ideal again, in order to realize that this wasn't Sleeping Beauty either, but a face that came marked with scars. If scenic action was a form of resistance, it seemed to extend itself into a time beyond the existence of the dictatorship and to realize that the option of art, since this conception, transformed itself into the metaphor of the no-response, like that question about existence.

## Art and Existence

We were born on a planet whose physical space was inhabited, where its couples aren't the originators, where each culture has transformed it in places. We were born on a planet where every territory already has an owner.

During our lives, we rent or buy the place we inhabit. We arrive in cities where the streets and parks have already been laid out, where the urban center is defined according to levels of ingress and egress. We choose the neighborhood that gives us the most access—depending upon either our inherited resources or those that we generate during our existence—to a range of possibilities, the beach or the countryside.

We don't define how our supermarkets are built, buildings are constructed or demolished, nor where parks, industries, or gas stations are placed. The objects to which we have access are already there, designed, elaborated according to their technological function, decorative nature, functional purpose, etc.

We won't reach the point of creating another civilization or another language during our existence. We arrive so that they can educate us to feel what exists is ours, "my country, my house, my language." During the years of our presence on this planet, we will, perhaps, be part of the appearance of other forms of dressing, living, governing or of influencing how a thought is inherited and other forms of knowledge are constructed. We can reorder objects, make them ours, re-elaborate their significance, project the concretion of our desires in our space-time and inhabit the diverse spirits of the age.

It's not a matter of rejecting or renouncing our species. On the contrary, we love it. We are part of it, and we assume responsibility for its errors and successes, we rebel against our evil and kindness. We nourish ourselves from our legacy, we have our own spaces, and we live according to our own emotions. We arrive to strengthen our culture, to reproduce it, to maintain it and to transform it, to reconstitute it with difficulty. We arrive at a planet where empires and economic systems are prevalent, and it is improbable that, during our passage our territory-nation will transform itself into a new empire and its action will produce the ways of seeing that will transform a planet.

But this is the imaginary of being human: its thoughts, its ideas, the creation of spirit that can give birth to non-existent fictions, speak and build from another dimension that isn't the quotidian, the material. That can create fictions out of emotions, and motivations as true as our gods. Finally, we are in a universe, and we confront death, and give impulse to feelings, that transcend whatever pre-existing empire or concrete modes of production, domination, or survival we find.

For the imaginary our fictions are realities, they are all at once the place to construct thought, the past and the future. The fictions of creation and artistic production gestate that other territory where our world can be reconstructed, deconstructed, and reformulated. From that place, we can say that the visions of our surroundings divulged by the media, the voices of politicians, of education, of the cultural values and beliefs in which we are immersed, lack, from our feeling, veracity. Where the logic of the discourses and thoughts that invade us, despite emerging from solid and consolidated structures, are only fictions for sustaining the space-time of the present.

The world transmitted to me, the world that I had to perceive, as well as the institutions that promulgated its ethics and its historical continuity, felt to me so far away from my perception of reality and its convictions, that creative forms transformed themselves into the place where I could resist and manifest my perceptions.

Artistic creation, its history, is where other places than the spaces of our existence register themselves. They transmit the reflection of imaginaries. We also know that we generate other perspectives and visions from artistic sites, some of them so formidable that they resituate the way the species looks at its material space, carrying us towards different paths than those prescribed. The creator reflects the species in its different dimensions and from different places and means.

We arrive at a space-time where art has its places and each one of its artistic expressions its own trajectory. The construction of humanity's fictions is also inherited baggage.

I am not postulating purifying or romantic ideas. Art and religion, as manifestations of the soul and the spirit, are not beyond good and evil.

We see priests blessing warplanes, battalions of soldiers—carrying medallions of the Virgin or saints—going to assassinate others of their species beneath the standards of national flags, some incriminating themselves for Allah and others for Jehovah.

We are surrounded by monuments glorifying generals and soldiers rewarded for their heroic massacres, or for having succumbed beneath enemy bullets on all the avenues of the great capitals.

The hero of the neighboring country is the enemy of the adjacent country.

Art also adds to the paradoxes of this reality; there is that of National Socialism, Stalinism, art of the market or of empire, conceived in connection to the money and fame that it brings with it.

Thus, each artist and religious person is rewarded and elevated to the altars for being in consonance with the spirits of the age of their culture. And those that reject the conceptions of their time will be sublimated because they resisted their age.

In our country, there are also artists who were faces or accomplices of the dictatorship, out of fear, for questions of labor, or because they were convinced that the regime was the best one for that historical moment.

I don't wish to make apologies for the correct or the incorrect, only to make our labyrinth plain.

There are also creators who subscribe to diverse ideological orientations, but who nevertheless contribute and reveal new paths of creation in their work, beyond their terrestrial ideological convictions.

Each new generation will emerge to align itself with what contains it or will have a passionate desire to transform it; perhaps they will reiterate, with each vote for existence, their love of nature, their hatred of war, and their feeling of solidarity. In others, their militancy for the destruction of what exists and for the eternal construction of a happy world will gestate.

The question becomes from which place will this happy world be visualized, and where will we situate the enemies of this glorious epic poem. We subscribe to a faith, its ideas, and motives and we can die for them, giving in this way a sense of existence. The reason for dying disturbs and changes: die for God in a colosseum, die for independence, die for territory, for your birthplace. Why die today? For art, executed by a firing squad, imagining some laurel wreath that descends in the hands of beautiful archangels.

We doubt the reason to die.

Power needs its art and its religion, and we need to survive for our religion and our art. Without doubt the role of the artist, in every age, is part of our history.

This essay's point isn't to submerge ourselves in these themes, but merely to enunciate them as points of reflection or confirmation. To signal that the creative way of seeing, the imaginary that materializes through the creative product, constitutes itself in a political way of seeing, and develops the politics of art.

That is to say, art generates politics as it constitutes itself in a culture of societies established with reference to identity, rebellion, or the manifestation of our emotions in the frame of an action.

It constitutes itself as a referent to action in our emotional relations, since these surface as experience from what came before; the representation of the body, the construction of thought through the structure of written language, all this leaves footprints on the ways we speak, think, and perceive.

Thus, this essay, like the plays and scenic presentations I've constructed, are for me in the end, part of a sense of life, a means of sensory resistance to elaborate the fictions of my perception as the mark of living in a time, a space, and on a planet.

# Atavism and Art

*Atavism: The tendency for the characteristics of more or less remote ancestors to reappear in human beings.*

That the gesture of desire constantly reappears throughout the process of being human is a fact that still surprises. Thus, today when someone dares to pierce or tattoo their skin, dyes their hair, makes up their face or undergoes cosmetic surgery, they are carrying out an atavistic gesture of the species. In what moment, whether as a sign of the tribe or of identity and difference, does the human being not make up their face, not perforate their earlobes, not tattoo their skin, or transform the desired structure of their feet or craniums?

The desire to dance around bonfires, in living rooms, in our own habitats, or in discotheques, to follow the rhythm of the music with our bodies, can be seen as an ancestral condition.

Without digging too deeply into the atavistic, we can look to our recurring dreams, which allow the existence of psychoanalysis and its efforts to figure out guidelines and signs of identity: the desire to fly, to possess, to dominate.

The species, distanced from the taboos of its religion or culture, allows its instincts to surface. Thus, the torture chambers and their instruments from the Middle Ages don't surprise us, nor do the atrocities of civil wars, the concentration camp at Auschwitz, the jails in Iraq, the Botswanan genocide, or the jailed and disappeared in Latin America. What they demonstrate is the mark of Cain. How we kill our brothers and are eternally condemned to an inheritance that generates assassination and wars as a reaffirmation of the species.

The eternal mea culpa of *Nunca Más* is like a confession; we mitigate the error, or we judge historical figures as the responsible demons, forgetting that behind them are institutions and citizens who defend life today and who didn't hesitate to pull the trigger yesterday. Leaving out the call "Never Again."

Generations will disappear justifying their actions and new ones will repeat them. The atavistic also contains love, desire, sexual pleasure, orgasm, and depression. We nourish ourselves from the atavistic in order to progress, desire and destroy. Undoubtedly it would be a bit simplistic to justify all our actions by inheritance, but we can't deny its potency.

Happily, to survive over time and, above all, in the present, we can erase the past in the face of the new necessities. It would seem that institutions, nations and tribes' survival instinct create forgetfulness or turns memories of the past into pain markers along a road that no longer exists. Forgetting and the search for happiness impedes our ability to perceive imminent tragedy. We only see it now that it flourishes, and it will never live up to our fantasies of it.

Those in my country today (today's defenders of the sacred institution of the family) who are kept up at night by the threat to life from contraceptive pills, yesterday permitted execution, kidnapping, and exile. And they have paragons in all latitudes and modes of thought.

Nevertheless, all that's gone before doesn't keep us from loving life, our existence, and our planet.

In this evolutionary process when a caveman painted a bison, a woman shaped a pitcher, or another built a flute, they repeated the desire to represent the immaterial dimensions that came to their minds, turning feeling into expression, that which today we call art. When an obelisk is raised or they sculpt faces on the walls of Tiahuanaco, the impulse is no different from that which built St. Peter's Basilica or the mosque of Al-Azhar.

Religion generates rites based in dogmas. Theatre generates rites for transformation, otherwise known as scenic languages. To represent ritual, construct signs, or decontextualize actions and words of the quotidian world, doesn't mean reiterating the tribal rites of anthropology or folklore, but points to those that arise out of the specificity of an action in eternal transformation.

The priest is the representative or actor of the divine. The actor is the representative of a mind in motion. The theatre needs to reconstruct its rites and its gods. We can sing in a church, express joy at a birth, in the same way that we laugh at the actions on the stage, sing with our actors, or cry at their tragedies. Some center themselves in the metaphysics of faith, others in the conventions of the truth of scenic representation.

Faith moves mountains, the theatre presents ideas that can become mountains.

The so-called division of labor in our social structures has maintained atavistic roles during its evolution, warriors to soldiers, shamans to priests, kings to presidents, buffoons to theatre companies, nobles to bourgeoisie, slaves to proletarians, tribe to village, village to nation.

Art has no answers, but reveals or insinuates paths towards them, so that a human nucleus makes them part of their culture or rejects them.

We can't claim that the nature of our life is predetermined. It is a mystery. It would be ingenuous to attribute it to predestination, like claiming that delinquency is an inherited condition.

The desire for religion is an atavistic impulse, the type of religion we choose is the institutionalization of this atavism: Christianity, Buddhism, Islam, Hinduism. Our atavistic behavior is institutionalized by the culture in which we are situated.

The atavistic impulse to collect and warehouse what we need to survive—food, clothing, tools—is the motor driving the market economy and the development of consumerism, made even more potent by means of advertising.

The atavistic warlike behavior of the Conquest, with its emphasis on possession and power, has been institutionalized in the existence of the Armed Forces. Where the fundamental cultural dictum "thou shalt not kill," produces exceptions in accord with whichever power and situation permits and delimits such an action. And the concept of art-artist is indifferently assumed within our mediatized culture—show business, commercial theatre, best seller—where the atavistic behavior of representing and going to see represented takes place in luxury, as part of the cultural industry, of the institutionalized consumption that leads to the social forms in vogue. Thus, the socially integrated art becomes that nucleus's culture of tomorrow.

Today's art will be tomorrow's culture, the foundation for developing that system's cultural politics.

The constant question is what of today's art will be tomorrow's culture? How is our ancestral atavism institutionalized today in the present?

When a country defends its patrimony yesterday's art is incorporated as culture. The artistic gesture, initially seen as subversive, is institutionalized and, as it is integrated into the culture, becomes part of a legacy and territorial patrimony. German Expressionism, Italian Futurism, Mexican Muralism, Dadaism, Huidobro's Creationism, ideological political theatre, etc. have all become part of how we construct knowledge, and essential referents in cultural and social diffusion and formation.

We find ourselves in a new context where we face a large quantity of artistic creations that, despite their construction of subversive ways of seeing, become disposable, don't succeed in establishing themselves, and aren't registered or disseminated socially, either because they are unknown or out of omission. This context is given to us by the "dictatorship mediated by the market" that doesn't disseminate such creations in its territory and that centers itself, fundamentally, around the diffusion of show business events or of market creations, both local and global.

Within the framework of a mediatized-globalized society freedom of expression disappears without dissemination. We can complete a play or write a book, but if there no means to disseminate it, we are generating thoughts and knowledge disconnected from their surroundings.

How can a citizen know about a work, or ask for a book, if they don't know it exists?

In today's context, mass media will never make us aware of these creations nor will the cultural patrimony, but the search for these sensibilities exists in us. It can be seen in centers of teaching, in academics who investigate and transmit the forgotten, as well as recording an action through virtual means.

Perhaps that phrase "art as tomorrow's culture" arose to give meaning to an action and the hope for its future valorization.

Perhaps the infinity of creations won't be tomorrow's culture, but their existence gives life to art, they develop languages and contribute to the construction of knowledge.

What concerns us is that the art of representation contains and expresses an atavistic gesture. As such, all we are doing is repeating an inherent gesture for a wish to survive beyond death.

This is where the manipulation of our atavisms, and the form in which we arrange and represent them differs from the way they have been institutionalized by society according to their value or validity for its patrimony.

The preceding is our theme given that The Dramaturgy of Space, in its initial premises, implies connecting ourselves with the atavistic alphabet of the gesture of scenic creation. Thus, scenic art, as an atavistic social gesture, cannot disentangle itself from this sociological prologue.

## Gestures of Expression or of Creation

Let me tackle the complex distinction between expression and creation, in order to explain when we are in the presence of one of these two acts.

Expression is the cultural use of theatricality, in individual acts or in popular demonstrations; and creation is the gesture that manifests itself through apprenticeship and the development of an artistic language.

This doesn't negate the inherent atavistic creative capacities of each individual, or the relationship that is generated between him and his work, but let's dig deeper for a definition that relates to our personal decisions in terms of an expression, our profession or life's dedication, as well as being an important pedagogical tool.

When do we transmit or come face to face with an expression or a creation? And which do we spread when? This is a relevant question for its implications in the "politics" or cultural definitions of different regimes. Expression and creation are forms that manifest themselves in the same way, but where gestures have different origins, objectives, and internal processes of development.

We all have the capacity to express ourselves, as a manifestation of the species, through the means our culture has given us. We can pass out flutes and tambourines to a group and we will generate musical expressions, ludic instants, and an internally expressive ambience. But that is a long way from mastering musical instruments or musical composition, or the ability to contribute to the creation of sonorous languages. We can all emit sounds from musical instruments. But without a previous knowledge of musical language it is impossible for us to compose a piano concerto. By the same token, we can all dance and we can be excellent dancers at parties, in discotheques, or at carnivals, but this doesn't make us choreographers or professional dancers.

From childhood, we can draw on paper or paint an individual or group mural on the walls of our cities. We can decorate our own rooms and urban spaces, creating decontextualizations of objects, colors, and texts, without necessarily becoming visual artists.

In carnivals, street festivals, and student parties we put on disguises, use make-up, and construct sets, expressing ourselves through these mediums, our critiques and our joys. By the same token, spontaneous or ephemeral events such as political rallies, sporting events, and other gatherings make use of theatrical codes to express themselves, without these acts constituting in the end a development of scenic art.

All of this has provided material for anthropology and/or sociology enabling us to decipher how the uses of the theatrical medium have manifested themselves in collective expressions. Undoubtedly, a Brazilian samba school can, on occasion, be more captivating and attractive than a theatrical work. These expressions are part of folklore and will constantly be repeated in traditional forms, corresponding to each culture and signaling expressions of identity.

I clarify this to make it plain to my reader where I am speaking from. In several seminars, I have found myself confronted by papers that talked about the development of Latin American Theatre using examples of our scenic development, without differentiating cultural or social expression from artistic creation.

Folklore's mission is memory and perpetuation and a regional dance, like all tradition expression, isn't meant is to be transformed or reinvented, but its elements can be the basis for the deconstruction of a scenic action.

I think that this confusion has more likely a populist character, since there is less risk to power in promoting folkloric expressions than artistic creations. There's a reason that dictatorships and populist regimes foment national folklore and consider it "popular" art.

Without doubt, there is a delicate relationship between emotion, expression, and creation. Let's imagine that we've asked a group to create a story about solitude. Someone gives us a piece of writing pointing out all the emotions, anguish, and tears that writing this prose piece has caused them, and emotionally reads us what they have written: "Oh, how alone I am, this lonely night, of tremendous solitude. Oh, how alone and solitary am I." We can't deny that they have realized an expressive gesture, but they haven't contributed to our perception of solitude, nor is their goal to establish a literary style. In the same way let's consider this theatre group that presents us with arduous work, carried out with dedication and full of emotions, but whose scenic texture gives us a television sketch. Or consider the street painter who offers us his seascapes or portraits and feels artistically discriminating.

These examples are totally valid in terms of expression, but in the face of a process that doesn't go beyond an expression, we can't clearly see them as popular creations.

They certainly exist and situate themselves in our memory or patrimony as such, but we must distinguish between when we are facing a cultural expression in artistic form or facing a gesture of creation.

Yes, a narrow relationship exists between the development of the arts in each location and the existing level of cultural expression there. Where the development of scenic art in a given location is more advanced, greater tools and levels are reflected in its social expression, and those expressions produce creative art. Whoever decontextualizes an artisanal weaving from its folkloric identity, placing it in other contexts, generates readings that go beyond the act of weaving towards a gesture where our readings and thoughts about this article are resituated, from the point of view of a specific language. In this way, an author can decontextualize folklore, transforming it from expression into creation.

## Virtuosity and Authorship in the Gesture of Creation

The constructive gesture called art is the result of productive work based on meanings, and this sentient action manifests itself through artistic gestures. The forms of production used by these gestures use a metaphoric alphabet for our idiomatic alphabet as the means by which to communicate with us. Thus, the history of the construction of each art's alphabet is the result of its particular artistic language.

The complexity of appropriating artistic languages in order to express ourselves depends upon whether the work that comes from them isn't anything more than the formal-cultural reiteration of a referent ascribed to an expression, or if we are realizing a creative gesture.

If you write a love story it will carry all the emotions and sensitivities present when it was written, but the form the story takes may be the result of a culturally learned format. Look, for instance, at the lyrics of some love songs, or the texts of some literary "best-sellers."

From there it follows that authorial creation is always a space to conquer. We must take the creative systems and concepts given to us, or the creative paradigms we are taught by our own culture, whether they are Socialist Realism, Franquista art, commercial art, etc., and discover ways to confront and reinvent those paradigms.

At the same time, in the labyrinthine universe of creative arts, we can detect those who opt for virtuosity of expression, or those who urgently seek to reformulate the same kinds of art to which they attach themselves.

A classical dancer can reproduce the steps and phrases that already constitute the language while giving it their own personality and still be a virtuoso of the discipline, just like a musician or musical interpreter whose choice is to interpret the great classic in a virtuosic manner. Thus, it will be the interpreter of Bach, but not the author of the composition, who will be a virtuoso. Without doubt a difficult and valuable artistic choice in the maintenance of a culture. Others, in their relationship with art, will center on the reformulation of their languages. Thus, contemporary dance will investigate the body in other spatial and kinetic compositions, as much as a musician will choose to reconstruct sonorous universes.

# Speaking from a Place: The Relationship between the Center and the Periphery

If it is true that scenic arts correspond in ideal terms to the collective space of humanity, it would be ingenuous not to point out that the contemporary world has defined, or wished to impose, certain territories or divisions—like the center—as the origin or supposed guides, to the advances or roads to follow in our evolution. Underscoring their power at the level of thought and discourse.

At the same time, they have confined peripheral territories to the role of efficient reproducers of these ways of looking at our universe.

The capacity for massive diffusion of the "cultural products" of the center across the globe, and the local incapacity—from the periphery—in situating its creators and its artistic history as an important place, both in terms of education and in its diffusion, incrementally increases the social sensation that local authorship is non-existent, both historically and in the present.

It's enough for us to point out that in our educational establishments, and even more so in the Western academy, the names and writings of our Latin American playwrights of the nineteenth century are unknown, and only a few from the twentieth century are recognized, and, consequently, our diverse conceptions concerning the same planet and our contributions to knowledge aren't integrated into the patrimony of our social formation and inheritance. These are replaced by discourses, symbologies, names, and epistemologies that come from the center, thus displacing cultural memory, annulling dialogues, and preserving hegemonies of knowledge.

Upon the occasion of Chilean independence in 1910, then President Manuel Montt pointed out that

> during the hundred years of independence the Republic is about to complete Chilean intellectual production, constitutes, as much for the number and variety of works as for the importance and substance of its materials, one of the most characteristic and honorable manifestations of national progress... This production is insufficiently known and appreciated inside the country and even less outside of it.
>
> (Nicolas Peña, *Teatro dramático nacional*, Santiago de Chile: Editorial Barcelona, 1912)

This was the impetus for the anthology *National Dramatic Theatre* in 1910. Its editor, Nicolás Peña, laments that he is unable to include the more than five hundred plays produced during this period. Plays that trace, through the Independence imaginary, our loves and our wars, which, if in the body of their passions don't differentiate themselves from those of the universal theatre, speak from unique events.

We can't be proud of an inheritance we don't know, or love what doesn't exist.

An anecdote: after the reading of *Cinema-Utoppia* in Berlin, a work of mine from 1985, a critic underlined the text's structural similarity to that of a play written by a German playwright in 1992, at which point I intervened, pointing out that the correct construction was that the German playwright's play was similar to "*Cinema*." This certainly wasn't an egoistic defense, but an attempt to redefine ways of seeing, by underscoring that not everything that comes from the periphery is a mechanical reproduction of ad hoc models from the center.

There exists a block, above all when it comes to the Latin American stage, against admitting that some creations from the periphery are autonomous authors who contribute to the development of scenic languages.

The colonial attitude is that we continue considering today's art according to the dictates of the center, assuming and divulging the notion that contemporary art is defined by and established by a festival or an exhibition in New York or Berlin, without understanding that our autonomy consists in constituting our own centers and places of reference.

Without a doubt, Western scenic creations offer common X-rays; text and staging, staging and text, trying to decipher signs repeated like a mirror, by a semiology overflowing in its enunciations. We can define the voices and images of our contemporary theatre by confronting that which has nourished us from the center.

Artistic actions manifest themselves in relation to the same Western theatre, but they see, they think, and they represent from other places.

Don't forget that from where we create, voices and images of a contemporary theatre are also generated. If they follow a similar format, we must also recognize that our voices have created other sounds and that our images arise out of other surroundings. The place from which we speak and create isn't the same place from which others speak.

And as a poetic objective, I hope that the voices and images of our contemporary theatre that arise out of different cardinal points are listened to mutually, and from this concert of sounds and visual images an understanding of theatre and, therefore, our action is deepened since we are the sparkle materialized that links millions of years that take shape in a present so ephemeral. From which it follows that the stage creator is nothing more than a spokesperson for their age, maintaining the fabrication of imaginaries.

We hold to the conviction that the sensibilities arising from different axes of the planet cause multiple perspectives of our reality to emerge.

I am the descendant of Italian immigrants with a Spanish great-grandfather who was a theatre musician in the middle of the Atacama Desert, the great-grandson of Chilean Diaguitas. Living in a twentieth century where one believed in and saturated oneself with this century's utopias, experiencing tyranny and exile, repeating the karma of exiles and tyrannies. Writing in a twenty-first century from a geography, between mountain ranges and the sea, is a hybrid constitution like so many others, nothing special in macro but distinct and determining in micro.

This little summary looks for the place to situate where one is born and the way that one constitutes to whom one writes. In a certain sense our personal biographies are linked to the histories of the world in which we live and from there is added the expression that a species develops to elaborate by means of an artifact, what constitutes the theatre: a space to speak, from other dimensions, artistic callings, what even now we can't decipher.

As unique is the place from where the planet's authors speak and find themselves in synchrony with the existence of the same global being. From there I underline writing from my territory, about an art of our species. It is the desire to contextualize the micro universe from which one writes and how from here we contribute to the stringing together or dissolution of an historical network whose direction we will never know.

This explains why The Dramaturgy of Space takes on the character of a glance at a common creational format and that the brief themes treated here aren't meant as a sociology of performance but rather reflections that have shaped a point of view.

# Art and Politics

The new contexts of institutional politics, a break from the ideologies to which some artistic models subscribed, lead to a profound change in the relationship between art and politics, resituating the creator's context, and the form and context of his creations.

We are at an historical crossroads, one where art can once more reflect its own politics, and where more deeply considered gestures of creation will give us more tools for the elaboration of its languages. This is not art for art's sake, that orthodox concept of creation as free from any discourse or contingent ideas other than its own.

During the twentieth century, a symbiotic relationship between political thought tied to society's fictions and ways to construct artistic realities was created.

In a period in which ideology was based on fiction, it made sense that art, itself fictitious, looked to ideology to nourish and produce it.

This led to theatre aligned with a particular ideology putting forth critiques based upon that ideology and promoting it. Either directly, as in the theatre of agitation and propaganda, or indirectly, informed by the structures of Marxist dialectics, anarchist thought, or the ideas of national socialism, among other examples.

Some theatre groups were previously political or social constructs and from there came the notion of a theatre collective as a partisan collective.

The members of theatre companies came together around shared theatrical aesthetics, and the plays they presented critiqued the systems they opposed and stressed the social message they wanted to promote. The historical continuity of the groups and the social-artistic framework they presented, brought together an audience in favor of their ideas and passions. In this context, some of the scenic expressions lacked an autonomous thought or way of seeing separated from the partisan utopian themes. Thus arose "popular theatres," assuming or appropriating each one of the people's ideas and defining for themselves what was a popular scenic expression, if they opposed bourgeois culture.

Since the art created was symbiotic with these ideals, there was scant artistic critique of those ideals. A critique from art of the utopia in question was incongruous, if it was realized in the face of systems that deviated from the approaches proposed as in the case of Mayakovsky against the system's bureaucracy. This led to the concept of the artist committed to the people's struggle, or of the popular artist; and to predetermining artistic models that corresponded to forms of creation that, for their textual poetics or their poetics of space, defined themselves as subversive.

## CHAPTER I

Inventing the slogan *"the new man"* requires a fictional representation of that slogan.

Thus, at the schematic level, language, characters, descriptions of exploitation, and their forms of representation, predetermine the form of creation. Since the left-wing Latin American scenic creator chooses texts and scenic forms whose iconography corresponds to the symbology and discourses of partisan politics beforehand, the creative process is blocked in some instances.

A clearer example is what happened with popular song in the 1970s in Chile. Each group, whether left or right, used the musical forms to give song a dissenting or conservative position. Thus, the folklore of the altiplano was taken up by the left and the social fiction of the present and the sounds of peasant tunes from the central valley were transformed into expression belonging to the right. Strictly speaking, none of these forms of folk music had a partisan origin.

Twentieth-century politics valued being aligned with art but annulled it and its creators if their work succeeded in expanding its imaginary beyond the margins of institutional politics, or if the artistic way of looking produced another reading of ideas and matrixes of the work.

As utopian ideologies for the future appeared art, searching for fictional constructions that transcend time, formed a natural alliance with them. This relationship operated as both a powerful motor of development and, many times, as a limit upon the expressive possibilities of its creators.

Today, when politics no longer proposes or represents alternatives that oppose the social fiction of the present, but only serves to administer the system in place, artistic alliance is no longer necessary. The system transforms art into a space for market culture, a space for commercial entertainment, or a place to dispose of free time. I understand commercial theatre as something born from profit not from the soul.

Art can retake the unvalued space of individual subjective expression, or of the solitary makers closeted with their own ghosts. As such, creative artists can dispel their energies in urban installations or interventions that can adorn our city before getting caught up in psychopathologies.

Thus, artistic creation, in the new context, can become social ornament. Performances or emerging artistic languages become marginal to the operation of the system. It no longer dirties its hands or its mind with proclamations that, upon passing from the imaginary to reality, only succeed in converting dreams into nightmares, in which art is left reduced to the role of mere accomplice in the construction of the dominant social systems.

Art divorced from the institutional political yoke, the creator liberated from imposed social compromise, challenges artistic language and finds itself challenged to make it represent and speak from its own sensory convictions.

No one delivers the slogan anymore. The reason to die.

We certainly can't claim artistic language is uncontaminated. Nor can we attribute liberatory and messianic powers to it. It does not purify society.

At one time, we thought that the theatre took spaces away from power. Today we want to think that it is the place of resistance to, and an antibody against, globalization.

Skeptically, we could say that art doesn't do anything more than register our states of being, stories, and discourses, providing fodder for the foundational facts of the social sciences.

Certainly, it is still the place to talk about death, about the emotion of a body in space, about the planet's existence, about the universe, about the meaning of life. About feelings that go beyond domestic facts and economic progress; themes that are absent from today's political discourse, which is even more disconnected from the motivations of art.

Art can take up again the continuity of its reason for existence, of always being the site for resistance.

Where the unique revolutionary consciousness that will liberate humanity from the yoke of consumption and work is the consciousness of death, which is the unconscious of artistic language.

We've arrived at one of the many limits of not believing in language, and, therefore, in the discourses that it elaborates. We doubt our thinking because we are betrayed by its practice. The scenic truth of discourse is destroyed while the structure or external relation-political—that justified or sustained it, the ideal of Utopia, continues existing in forms of representation called imaginary, but that never become an operative reality, since the species' incapacity to realize its desire in social order has become a constant or the only way to be or exist.

Christ's words, like those of Marx, are finally nothing more than desires. And each mistaken elaboration by human beings of those desires will be seen as erroneous practices. But we will maintain our faith in the fiction that proposed them. It would seem, then, that only in fictional spaces can the social desires of thought materialize. The political struggles of the twentieth century weren't anything more than attempts at fictional representation in mistaken contexts of creation.

When I listen to real speech, I feel like I hear scenes from plays. Like all fiction, some seem full of commonplaces and others dig deeply in word and action. It's precisely at this point that the ambiguous swarm of what I'm talking about emerges, the unnecessary discourse of knowing where we limit the subjectivity of objectivity or, to put it another way, when are we in one space or in another, and according to whose way of seeing?

I understand who I want to communicate with by means of art, like someone looking for a method of communication no one owns, and who wants to appropriate an instrument to use, as an autonomous method of communication.

Expression from the place of the imaginary is not disconnected from what exists. Nor from the history or the spirit of the age it inhabits. It is only a language that arises out of the history of each artistic expression. Whoever talks about love, or their relationship with their father, talks about their own existence, about a family, and a common desire, to the inhabitants of this planet.

During our temporal existence, it's impossible to talk from an extraterrestrial imaginary. This is why that "imagination" of the artist is a fallacy, since the artist does imagine, but based on the re-elaboration of codes and experiences from their surroundings and the structure of the continuity of an artistic language.

But without doubt, it was the relationship between art and politics that pulled the trigger on a profound, intense, and magnificent development of creational languages in the twentieth century. That has left us enormous knowledge, which will be re-elaborated in new contexts where art will construct its own politics.

Our theatre today can be perceived as a politics of art established using diverse views and poetics of space unfurling in a manner that no longer adheres to the concept of political art from the twentieth century. One of the many examples of this are the demonstrations that took place during our social rebellion in 2019 when the street was transformed into a stage. You no longer went to hear someone up on a platform. Social groups demonstrated by means of literature, writing on the city's walls, through choreography, art actions, theatricalities, music, songs, digital expressions cast upon the building's walls, where party slogans or banners were absent. For me, this expression demonstrated the politics of art, appropriated by the people in what I would call social creation. This collective art appropriation was nourished by the historic interactions between creators and citizenry.

# Earlier Scenic Models and Original Authorship

*The move from photocopy to original authorship provides the perfect opportunity to reformulate theatricality, enabling us to profoundly change our ways of seeing, thinking, and transgressing.*

The twentieth century was characterized by a collection of thoughts that defined perceptions of our surroundings and reality in accord with paradigms or models that became addictive and whose passionate force is missed by some today.

The largest ideological models of industrial capitalism (Marxism, Fascism, Anarchism) materialized as visions of the surrounding world. They generated artistic models inspired by the imaginaries of those visions, adhering to the ideas and utopias proposed by their models. Without a doubt, the historic failure of those visions led to the breakdown of the truth of their explanations and, consequently, in the failure of the artistic truths of their imaginary expressions.

Stage representation wasn't divorced from the construction and definition of models in line with the particular codes constituted by them. Since they were created with their own rules, in accord with those of their founders or the movements from which they came, the walls erected by these models impeded their fusion or integration.

Different paradigmatic artistic visions prevented Symbolism and Naturalism, or Expressionism and Psychological Realism, from combining.

Latin American artists mainly added to these models from the center. Consequently, all the definitions for stage art coming from these models can only be understood in relation to the paradigms that formed them. The categories they provide can't be used to define new artistic languages and are largely useless to us as references.

Such stage models were constructed as totalities, paradigmatic. Symbolism implied a particular dramatic structure, an emotive bodily form of acting from the soul, a particular form of stage composition (lighting, music, costuming), and scenery that constituted a universe.

Realism also implies a form of staging, a dramaturgical use of objects, a scheme of dramatic writing, a form of character construction, and a way to construct the narrative of the space. Briefly put, each movement creates a set of rules that leads us to the construction of a fictional convention.

Thus, as we will go into more deeply later, talking about Realism in relation to the model, is not the same as conceiving of a realistic work disconnected from that paradigm, since the appropriation of *reality* for the stage is a twentieth-century arbitrary act that sets aside as unrealistic all prior and subsequent playwriting as non-realistic expressions, deauthorizing the construction and vision of reality of other authors.

When Konstantin Stanislavski proposes the foundations for a twentieth-century theatricality, he is generating a model in opposition to, or as a re-elaboration of, the scenic fictions that preceded him. The Baroque theatre, for example. Thus, when we attend a version of *Hamlet* that follows this model, we aren't attending the most truthful form of representation of this text, but only an interpretation of it made for model in question.

The stage identity of the twentieth century is constructed, then, by the appearance of multiple models, each of which is looking for the most faithful representation of the human spirit in stage fiction and which, generally, is in artistic opposition to the existing or preceding models. In the meantime, artistic conceptual foundations and the form of perceiving scenic truth for each one is autonomous in relation to the others.

The theatrical training that emerges in universities or conservatories after the Second World War chooses, according to their directors, to transmit or perfect prior curricular models. In Chile, university theatre schools chose the model of Psychological Realism, centering on the study of Stanislavski and his followers, considering it as the most contemporary approach to the stage, influenced by its large resonance in North American centers of study. The tools developed by "the Method," in its concept of Psychological Realism, are indisputably tailored to film acting in a country where the film industry requires that kind of actor training.

This type of training put the brakes on the creation of local methods as it centered itself on learning already-established gestures of creation with virtuosity. Studying whichever method already contains within it a form of fictional construction and, therefore, the construction of space and of acting forms.

*Learning* how to build a theatrical language wasn't transmitted: rather, how to *reproduce* one. Despite all the variations of distance, language, and actors' bodies, we sought to recreate it on our stages. Even more, theatrical training was centered on the search for stage truth, a logical concept in a moment where the truth (ideological-scenic) was defined as correct in the face of the incorrect.

I am not expressing a criticism or value judgement, only offering an X-ray of the state of things in coherence with the spirit of the age.

A scenic model was considered the template or paradigm for a director who defined himself/herself as a faithful follower of that model, interpreting it through their political and dramatic vision. Thus, "a Brechtian man of the theatre" will consider it a success if his production is recognized as a creation that perfectly complies with the postulations of the model in question. We could say that he succeeds in becoming a virtuoso in this method of creation.

The entire vanguard of the beginnings of the twentieth century constituted itself around subversive artistic actions that confronted institutional models. Voices that wanted to manifest themselves with proposals that rejected the preceding theatrical currents ability to interpret reality.

Through their manifestations and creations, they invited subscription to new models, more efficient for revealing reality, more creative, more subversive, and as forms of expression of a present and a future necessary for the new man and the new art that would be disclosed by utopias in battle or in construction.

They evolved in relation to the break from scenic truths tied to ideological truths, and other authorial forms with new scenic gestures to which one could subscribe were generated. In this context figures like Eugenio Barba, Arianne Mnouchkine, Jerzy Grotowski, the Artaudian renewal, etc. stand out. In Latin America, instead of incentivizing the creation of our own universes these forms of creation from the center were mainly reproduced.

These languages inscribed themselves in an ideological imaginary, but they shouldn't be reiterated and frozen in time, defending a pre-existing scenic convention, for that reason alone.

In the context of the end of the twentieth century the evolution of thought and perception puts some of the established conventions about scenic truth, methods of representation and of ordering the signs in space, and, most fundamentally, the ways an actor interprets a text and emotion, as well as the hieroglyphic gestures that carries with it, into crisis.

The loss of the truth of a model manifests itself in a reading distanced from its aesthetic, in which the theatrical artifices are left revealed while commonplace statements are transformed into archetypes that demythologize what is represented. As a result, the (pseudo) re-reading serves as parody. In this process, the forms of construction of its decontextualization lose the force of their fictional truth and are phased out of the perceptions of the present. Scenic truth is no longer the domain of a movement but has become schizophrenic. This is the favored moment, since breaking the boundaries of a convention allows theatrical creation to emerge.

Perhaps instead of generating our own gestures that depart from the theatrical format and the sum of theatrical languages that have been generated, we have centered theatrical development more upon the continuation and perpetuation of inherited models.

In my early works during the 1980s I could certainly admire and nourish myself from all this accumulated theatrical inheritance. I had no desire to be the virtuosic expression of a predetermined model in my writing and staging but aspired to metaphysical impulses and personal passions that constructed their own perceptions of reality or their own fictions. Having read a brief essay by Oskar Schlemmer (1888–1943) about scenic deconstruction in order to create the theatre of the new man by returning to initiatory rites to activate a performance in order to understand its format, its geometric conceptions, body, color, and sound, I found concordance with my vision to make the theatrical gesture comply with the fundamentals of visual narrative; to write about and from the space, allowing the creative gesture to emerge from the matrixes of the alphabet of the scenic language and not from a previously constructed model.

The scenic models used in those years—and, in many ways, still today—were structures already elaborated on top of the scenic format. Theatrical training didn't give you the tools to construct fictions from the space, but to reproduce gestures and languages already constructed and imposed upon it. But those models had a point of origin, that of work related to the alphabet of a theatrical language, situated in the first instance in relation to the stage format, which is the space and its visual narrative.

Because the space doesn't carry *a priori* any ideology or form of elaboration, it is only a place for the decontextualization of its own universes.

Everything given to us by artistic movements of the twentieth century, as well as those before, undoubtedly constitutes our database, our historical references, and allows us to develop our skill and diverse creative languages. Today they can no longer be perceived as theatrical truths to reproduce, but as references for creation, from which we should certainly nourish ourselves and utilize their contributions and discoveries, regardless of the paradigm that contains them.

The dramatic text in this way is left disconnected from the performative model to which it subscribed, no one can determine the correct poetics of space in which to perform a Greek, Elizabethan, or contemporary text. A particular production of *Life Is a Dream* can't be offered as the official version of its performance. Neither is the dramatic structure of the Absurd, Psychological Realism, or a conceptual text the manual for correct dramatic writing.

From the 1950s to the 1970s several of our directors traveled to countries in the center to learn the versions in vogue of such and such a text in order to return to produce them in their countries of origin, believing that in this way they brought the contemporary and up-to-date forms of art from which one had to nourish oneself to their own territory. Thus, the Experimental Theatre at the University of Chile vaingloriously claimed that their production of *Death of a Salesman* in 1950 was identical to that realized in New York in 1949. Its director would admiringly describe to Arthur Miller, during his visit to Santiago decades later, how he had attended the original production and made sketches of the scenery and the staging in order to reproduce them.

Strange pride in our theatrical ability to reproduce the milestones of modernity. Perhaps a necessary process to engender future creative work. I am pointing out a dominant tendency and not denying the isolated existence of creators who did try to propose other theatrical options.

The texts are there to be re-performed, to be re-visited, but they don't come with a recipe for their form of construction, the building of character or their set design. Playwriting pedagogies adjust themselves to indications in agreement with the scenic possibilities of the age, reinterpreting its spatial poetics to protect the textual poetics, that which is essential in its dialogues, retorts, and the universe it gives us.

Our emotions and sensations will trigger these texts for us. From their concordance with our mystical-political and existential passions, and our own visions about performance will emerge the poetics of spaces and the acting typologies of the production will be realized, since the continuity of scenic creation is the constant re-claboration of the codes of its own theatricality. Nobody can arrogate to themselves the way of seeing the imaginary, nor the form in which a work should be performed; that contravenes the practice of art itself.

We live in a pivotal period. One where the artistic visions and the teachings of modernity coexist. One where the scenic languages that correspond to models from stage history are learned so that we can reproduce them, or build upon them, alongside the postmodern spirit that postulates the generation of creative works apart from artistic inheritances and the particular emotions that confront them, and where the motor of creation emerges out of the place or territory of each creator.

A modernist critic, for example, will evaluate a performance in terms of the analytic categories that the epistemology of modernity elaborated. This prevents them from diverse perceptions of a work that doesn't adjust itself to the codes that come from this theoretical frame. They always have to adjust the productions in reference to their analytic canons and in relation to preceding models.

Thus, postmodern works, when viewed from the perspective of modernism, are left restricted to an analytical paradigm in respect to how a character should be, how conflicts should develop, how the work is structured and what style it uses, preventing them from being seen and re-read in accord with other creative gestures and another analytical nomenclature of gestures of creation emerging from scenic authorship, such that we are obliged to generate concepts to redefine them and not vice versa.

The classical concept is one in which praxis generates theory, and then it is confronted by praxis.

# Decontextualization as the Premise for a Fiction's Perception

The first gesture of artistic creation is the act of decontextualization. From reality we extract color, a body, an object, the word, and situate them inside of a format and a defined artistic language that begins to be perceived or read based on this gesture.

With spatial narrative, photography decontextualizes the space and situates it inside of its viewfinder. Film reproduces the same gesture. The visual artist extracts color, gives it form, configures it on a canvas or a space, and generates their creative act.

Different ways of constructing gestures of decontextualization define the differences between the arts, their styles, and aesthetics. While decontextualization of whichever element of our surroundings is the first step in the construction of an artistic language, the basis of its mechanics of creation provides the means of elaboration.

The theatre situates a body on the stage, thereby converting it into an actor, someone who performs: this body begins to narrate and generate signs and movements considered fictional by the convention that generates their decontextualization. We extract an object, situate it inside a space next to a body thereby constructing a visual narrative, a poetics of space.

From this point of view, the evolution of stage art is the history of infinite gestures of decontextualization that narrate how we have represented in space bodies, words, designs, scenery, lighting, music, or sounds.

The phenomenon of the act of decontextualization generates its own reality and its own communicative language. The classification of this action is part of the memory and the history of the language of performance.

So much so that a body in space emitting a sentence from its bodily movement, as much as the scenic actions that it creates on the stage, constructs its own grammar from its decontextualizations.

The gesture and the way in which we decontextualize will be considered in relation to its quality, skill, reference, or authorship, if it will refer us to constructions from scenic memory, or if it will generate stage representations that contribute to structuring other forms of decontextualization that allow us to see emotions and situations from other places, it will produce a change in our perceptions about the visuality and the orality represented.

By means of this rituality we distinguish reality from fiction. By means of the convention generated we situate it inside the spatial format of the site of our decontextualizations.

We are familiar with innumerable art actions based upon the annulment of this division between fiction and reality in order to generate other perceptions on the part of the audience. We situate the spectator in front of an action that he should perceive as not preconstructed. Since he is not in a decontextualized place, we point him towards another type of perception. Concepts like Agosto Boal's *invisible theatre*, where a prearranged conflict arises in a public space, are clear examples of these experiences.

But whatever act in which we generate a representation in a space—theatres, museums, stadiums, movie theatres, urban interventions—is centered on the process of constructing a decontextualization, generating from that its own convention. As spectators, we aren't part of the film or the play, unless they interpolate us and make us part of it based on our feelings and the way in which they appropriate the action.

The temporal space of a creative work doesn't correspond to our present dimension, but to the dimension of our feelings and memory. It is this process of decontextualization that initiates the process of creation and where we can perceive the language of art.

The convention used gives existence to another dimension, that of art or religion, and, via decontextualization, opens another place in which to read our thoughts and perceptions. Our sensory and psychic construction, according to the place that generates their decontextualization, allows us to give different value or truth to our perceptions.

This is the point where art and religion unite.

Faith is a convention, a truth about a fiction, in this case of religious character. Art is another convention about the reality of its fiction. Social utopias and religions establish the same relationship between being and idea; for both truths, you must be ready to martyr yourself.

Art constructs fictions, a stage performance redirects our sensations and emotions, we cry about deaths that aren't. We hate characters and can change our ideas or values about facts, and social relations, and develop ourselves.

The representation of the imaginary has elaborated different places for its existence. There are fictions that become eternal, like classical plays, but the challenge—and that differentiates them from religious decontextualization based upon inalterable dogmas—lies in the fact that art must reconstruct different constructions and imaginary poetics at each stage in its evolution, reinventing conventions to realize the imaginary of the age it is representing and to reconstruct its scenic truth. The text of *Antigone*, for example, re-acquires its mysticism and its fiction in this process of re-elaboration of scenic conventions.

As for someone wanting to culturally establish the fiction of a new religion, the question becomes one of definition: who defines the fiction of art or determines the tendencies of contemporary art.

Historically, Western and Eastern empires defined or elaborated fictional and artistic truths as the value systems and structures of power. Thus, our notion of fiction refers to the moment in which we perceive the phenomenon of decontextualization and let ourselves be guided by the language it is creating, giving emotional truth to this game we have invented.

A rite from Bali or an African religious dance is not fiction for those who perform it but, since we don't hold that faith's conventions, nor recognize its codes, we assign it theatricality based upon our ways of seeing.

Religiosity, rites of initiation, or folklore aren't in their contexts, or for their participants, scenic experiences, nevertheless, for us they revisit the form of spectacle. The orthodox priest doesn't use a costume, calls to prayer emitted from minarets aren't operatic arias, devils confronting the Virgin aren't scenic gestures, they are ritual gestures that inspire our scenic fictions.

Yes, we aspire to a scenic act that carries the emotional truth of a ritual.

## The Scenic Space and its Support

The space is the basis of our act of decontextualization. It is where we form the scenic language, where we generate the poetics of space that are established and articulate the narrative of the textual poetics.

A *priori*, the space contains no predetermined form as to how it should be constructed. At its base the space is a place without ideology, without content, without voice or image. It is only the foundation for a convention and a language. Each approach to constructing a fiction in the space lacks any predetermined manual. Previous models are nothing more than references of how representation has been done in the space.

The space supports the format of scenic creation. The reflections proposed here, and their exercises, are one of many ways to approach it. The stage space is marked as the place for performance, one that unites concepts of space and format.

One must distinguish that the stage is a spatial site where a dramatic manifestation is produced and that is defined by its placement or the architecture that contains it. Its location doesn't depend only upon it being inserted into a theatre building, but also on the place or places where the creator situates the fiction.

It can be, therefore, at one and the same time the façade of a building, a street, a bodega, gardens, woods, classrooms, a circus tent, a room, and/or a proscenium stage. Places as infinite as the material spaces we've constructed. The scenic space can be diverse imagined places or places to be imagined.

It is fundamental to recognize that the geometric nature of the spatial format that we have historically adopted to capture our artistic-cultural expressions is rectangular. The rectangular geometry of that format has led to the artistic visual narratives that we have developed.

# The Rectangle as Format in the Age of Social Rectangularization

We have defined the basis of the stage as its space, now we will defend the thesis behind its format, which is the geometric figure of the rectangle.

We hold that the West has chosen the rectangular form for projecting the dimensions of our thoughts. Diverse manifestations, be they spiritual, mediated, functional, urban, quotidian, object-based, etc., have developed out of the rectangular figure.

We encounter the rectangle beginning with the rectangular nature of classrooms. Where teaching is transmitted beginning with the blackboard. We then read rectangular books that contain the history of our knowledge. The daily information we receive comes in rectangular newspapers, where the advertisements and the news they offer us are inside of other little rectangles.

We place ourselves in front of our television so that, from that rectangle, we perceive thousands of rectangular frames that transmit to us advertisements, news, series, political acts, and festivals.

We hang our rectangular pictures on our rectangular walls in our rectangular rooms. We frame our nearest countryside by means of rectangular windows, we look at our rectangular calendars, we repose on top of our rectangular beds and, finally, our bodies lie in repose in a rectangular coffin in the rectangular church, to be deposited in a hole in the ground or a niche of the same format.

Designers draw their posters on rectangular planes and the large advertising billboards that fill our avenues, highways, and metros emerge from the same plans. We place ourselves in front of the rectangular screen of our computer to navigate the virtual world of the internet, overflowing with infinite sites and giving us this virtual universe through compositions inserted into this geometric form.

We plow and harvest in rectangular fields. Our urban planning divides our space into squares, installs green spaces of the same form, and sites of power establish themselves in large architectural rectangles.

Finally, the patriotic symbol of almost all the countries on the planet is imprinted on a rectangular piece of cloth. We could argue that the rectangle is the predominant functional form. However, what most calls our attention is that most artistic languages, and visual narratives, have developed inside of this format.

The plastic arts express themselves on rectangular canvasses. Through the rectangular viewfinder of a photographic machine or cellphone we register an image, and we go to movie theatres to see projected, on rectangular screens, the different fictions of their authors. We fragment our comprehension and perception of temporal and visual narrative in relation to this sequence of projections and attend dance, music, and theatre inside of this rectangle.

In this context our visual artistic experiences only echo the existing social rectangularization. By appropriating from this format they reflect their age, recreating in miniature the great rectangular matrix, whether as a mirror of our environment or constructing parallel dimensions and other spatial temporal narratives that permit the confrontation between existing fiction and other fictions that emerge from scenic, cinematic, or digital rectangles carrying with them an autonomy that transforms them in a place of unconscious collectivity born of knowledge, criticism, and, therefore, in a political space.

The major phenomenon that forms our perception and notion of the world assigns us to the geometry of the rectangle.

I have perceived two axes that bring us to this condition. One is that the frame realized by our organic vision, which, although it is ellipsoidal, has its defining margins that conform to a rectangle. The other refers to the argument that the human being creates the world in its own image and likeness. This interior psychic vision is what we materialize in the form already expressed.

The rectangle of our vision—its symmetry, its depth, its planes—is, therefore, formally, what we have evolved in our visual narrative and in our capacity to read it by means of our cultural, psychic, and sensory perception. All of which forms how to learn the compositions constructed there and the signs that they elaborate. Later we will see how this perception also affects our notion of space-time.

I haven't found any writing that references the determining specifics of this evolutionary phenomenon, or that points to the conditions that caused us to abandon our circular perception, to subscribe to a notion of the world centered on the rectangle.

In Athens, the Parthenon, with its marble rectangle sitting on the peak of the Acropolis, will be the most significant initiatory monument in the rectangularization of Western civilization. This can also be seen in the *skene* of the Greek theatre.

We live on a circular planet, lit by a circular sun, and circular trajectories of the atoms that are our essence form us.

But it is the rectangle, omnipresent geometric figure, that surrounds us and establishes itself as the global visual format.

## Of the Circular

Nevertheless, we know that in their origins many human cultures cleared the geography of their territory in circular form, from the igloo to the Atacama towns to the African steppes, it was the circle that prevailed in the construction of their habitats.

The cosmos they confronted was the celestial vault—circular—their gods were suns and moons. And they sat in circles to discuss fundamental themes or eat around the bonfire or pray with their leaders. When hunting they dispersed in circles to stalk their prey. There was a relationship habitat–religion–rituality around the circular.

We could put the circular temple of Stonehenge up against the rectangle of the Parthenon, as two great representations of both perceptions. As well as the circular calendars—Maya, Hindu, Chinese—for the ordering of time against our oblong or rectangular calendars.

When and how did we become separated from our circular condition? Was it when we broke our organic union with nature? Was it when the human being, in its evolution, stopped perceiving or feeling like the animals that we primarily are? Is it the product of civilization, a psychic change, where the axis of our relationship to the cosmos and nature—where rectangular forms are absent—is displaced and internalized apart from our own physiological construction?

The circular buildings for representation that we construct allow the reproduction of an animal's territorial perception. The Roman Colosseum could contain lions, tigers, horses, bears, allowing them to move inside of their own organic space. The bull ring, with its circular form, allows the bull to feel itself in its space and be able to attack. The Chilean rodeo, with its half-moon circle, makes the running of cows and horses possible. The same thing happens with the circular space of cockfights, and with the corral, the place for domesticated animals, and, finally, the circus ring that facilitates the presentation of tamed animals.

It is difficult for us to imagine a rectangular circus. Even the ideal fishbowl should continue its oval shape and avoid the rectangular aquarium more suited to our homes.

Our other circular spaces for entertainment, like sports stadiums, are organized so that we can better contemplate the rectangle where the action takes place, such as the rectangular field for soccer, field hockey, the basketball court, or the Olympic pool.

I will not expand upon the thousands of examples that confirm this premise, nor is it the point of this work to dig into the evolution of this form in terms of the format taken by our cultural expression. The foregoing simply seeks to confirm, reaffirm and, from there, try to comprehend the way in which we construct fictions inside of the rectangle.

And, at the same time, to recognize nostalgia for the loss of the circle, and attempts to recuperate it in friendly spaces, atavistic, to reunite with the circle, in therapy or in certain garden designs...

# History of Art and Rectangular Composition

Seen another way, the history of art can be approached depending upon the way we give form to our content within the rectangular space. This establishes a chronological history of styles seen from this perspective.

For example, when we enter a museum and stroll through its galleries, the various time periods are evident by the artists' use of color and the figure as they compose their work within the rectangle. We can clearly distinguish a Romantic painting from a Cubist one, a kinetic piece of art, or an abstract one depending upon the creative gestures realized in the rectangle.

Thus, so-called visual culture, seen as the new contemporary literacy, arises from the capacity to perceive readings, identifications and associations in the composition of our visual constructions. By the same token, the forms, letters, and compositions of graphics and publicity posters defines how we have perceived the medium since its inception.

If we had a registry of all the productions in history, we could recognize the period each creative gesture corresponded to by how lighting, gesture, acting, and scenic compositions were represented in the space, enabling us to catalog the history of the poetics of space, and take an X-ray of its age.

In fact, even the scarce graphic and photographic history of performance allows us to recognize a vaudeville theatre from its images, and we distinguish it from a constructivist, conceptual, or psychologically realistic theatre.

## The Stage Space and the Theatre Building

The architectural design of the theatre building developed in concert with the largest moments or constructions of its age. The theatre building correlates to the civilization's level of development and shows how it responds to the political and religious constructs that surround it.

In this way, the theatre building—which contains the rectangular format for performance—was constituted historically as part of an architectonic relationship with the palace, the church, the stage building, the government, or the town hall. It is still common to see in our cities, heirs to the colonial Spanish organization, the outline of a square with its church, town hall, and theatre.

We can trace a cultural parallel between church-temple, palace-castle-lord's mansion, and the stage building as part of the same visual symbol of cultural representation.

The classic marble temple, its staircases, its imposing rectangular space, its materiality, its frescos and sculptures, is reiterated in the Greco-Roman theatres in their marble materiality, their arched entrances, their sculptures, that are the backdrop to the stage. The Western Middle Ages created their castles with feudal architecture, containing large spaces and half point arches, coarse, dark, and out of cold stone. The same construction reproduced and developed by Western Christian Romanesque or Gothic churches.

The theatre is absent from this European Medieval period, given that as heir to popular and pagan traditions opposed by the patrons of Christianity, the theatre occupied a culturally conflicted place (dramatic art seen as the unpleasant aftertaste of a polytheistic culture).

And, nevertheless, it will be in front of the rectangle of the altar that we will see performance emerge once more by means of the *auto sacramentales*, or it will be in the cathedral courtyards where the large stages for the mystery plays will be constructed.

In front of the facades of these churches—baroque, gothic—lush with gargolylic, naturalistic, or corporeal representations, stage performance emerges again, perhaps as an elaboration of those petrified sculptures, as if the presence of those figures constituted a theatrical preamble that demanded their materialization.

Thus, the Roman theatre façade with its three doors appears again in the church façade with its three doors. The ephemeral mobile rectangles of the mansion stages or allegorical carts never constituted theatrical buildings.

In the Renaissance, with the Venetian Teatro Olímpico in 1580, a theatre building is constructed once more. Andrea Palladio, its architect, impregnates it with the façade of a Renaissance prince's palace reminiscent of the basilica of the same city. Shakespeare's Globe Theatre, constructed in 1599, reflects the architecture of the great houses of the Tudor lords.

Aside from the distribution of the audience, they all protect the rectangle as the center of the theatre space. Thus, successively, we see that in Neoclassicism the palaces of Versailles are reproductions of the great churches of their age, with their *trompe-l'oiel* paintings, their bronze candelabras, and their marble columns. The same concept pervades the so-called Italianate theatres with their balconies, large salons, candelabras, and painted ceilings.

In Santiago de Chile, our first colonial church, San Francisco, with its large walls of red adobe, wooden windows, and tile roof reflects to us the manor house of the large-estate owners from the central zone of our country. I don't have references, but it is conceivable that the first theatre buildings were also made of adobe and tile. Our cathedral and neoclassical churches, like the aristocratic palaces of the nineteenth century, have a similar architecture to that of our first theatre buildings, like the Teatro Victoria in Valparaíso and the Municipal in Santiago. Finally, we remember the Teatro de Iquique, that with its architecture of Oregon pine, recalls the house of the saltpeter industrialists.

By the same token the city theatre in Brasilia de Niemeyer finds its reflection in the cathedral of the same city. This fact isn't only a Western phenomenon. The mosque, with its worked mosaics and geometric figures is a simile for the sultan's palace, and the Confucian or Buddhist temple a simile for the emperor or mandarin's palace. And we see these cultural architectonic identities reproduced in their theatre buildings.

In Communist or Fascist regimes as well the theatre building's architecture reflects the architectural monuments of those systems. Even the pocket theatres of the 1950s and 1960s reflect the middle-class habitat of those times. The way power represents itself influences the development of architecture as a constant refrain.

The theatre building follows the same parameters as the building of power, until performance, looking for alternatives, elects new places for representation—sheds, shops, subterranean tunnels—that allow other approaches for the development of a creative gesture, or are chosen because it is impossible to give in to the demands of institutional architecture.

We hold that the use of an alternative space for performance, that at one time could have been realized as an artistic choice against institutionalization, an act of subversion, is today determined more by creative choice. The decision to present a play in a non-conventional space—the metro, a house, a factory, a plaza, or a circus tent—no longer implies by itself a renovation of theatrical language.

Today we can find ourselves facing reiterative creations, inspired by worn-out languages, in a shed as much as in a bourgeois theatre building.

Since the diversification of theatre practice is part of today's cultural politic—taking theatre to fields, neighborhoods, towns, or urban spaces—the political act of choosing a stage space is defined more by the politics of the art and established more by the discourse and theatrical act that implies. Today the relationship between the theatre building and its time no longer carries with it an association between stage creation and social symbology or the historical origin from which the stage space emerges.

Nevertheless, the choice of the space in which to perform can still signal a mark of artistic differentiation. Even democratic systems don't put all institutional spaces at the disposition of all creators. Personally, I find it difficult to choose stages located in commercial centers, although this may be nothing more than resentment towards the "mercantile" iconography of these places and the consequent identification with a market ideology that choosing them implies.

When a given period of ideological politics ceases to exist, the theatre building is no longer a simile for the power palace but simply another place for creation. One that also doesn't define the quality of its repertory.

In situations in which dictatorships or authoritarian regimes establish themselves again, the theatre building, as the city's landmark, can return to being the site of performances and censorships that express the power in vogue. Thus, the Teatro Municipal in Santiago, our Opera House, became, during the dictatorship, the place for galas and celebrations of the regime.

At the beginning the theatre building, in concert with its stage construction—boxes, footlights, stage machinery—only allowed certain types of performances to be realized in that space. Today, the stage machinery or technology is no longer determined by the theatre building, since we now have giant moveable stages that can be reinstalled in urban spaces, in many cases with dimensions that no theatre building can contain. Due to the culture industry and market price these giant stages aren't part of the daily life of theatre art, but more of market spectacles, industrial music, and recitals, etc.

At the same time, the stage space within multiple urban interventions can appropriate whatever architecture installed for its performance, always recreating the rectangular space, mentally, to generate its spatial narrative. Be it because the visible stage has fixed boundaries, be it because a lack of boundaries allows the amplest composition for the chosen space, the rectangular frame will be reiterated on many planes, in a manner inherent to the structure of a visual narrative.

Clearly, all creation whose work is eminently subversive in the face of the dominant fiction will have to reinvent its forms of production and sites of performance.

# CHAPTER II

## Approaches to The Dramaturgy of Space

From what was expressed in the first chapter comes the following correlation of ideas:

a) Theatre defines itself as an atavistic act, the culture where it is inserted institutionalizes this act giving it a context in which to manifest itself. The creative gesture, enacted, breaks away from the limitations that cultural systemization has established, re-elaborating its languages to distance itself from that institutionalization, and establishes once more its autonomy of expression.

b) Contemporary partisan politics, upon ceasing to be representative of the concepts of the existence of humanity, abandons in its discourse proposals that confront existential notions of being—death, the universe, desires, the notion of happiness—as well as constructions for tomorrow's social fictions, or the capacity to imagine other socio-political orders. In this context, art reconstitutes itself as the place to construct and continue these notions, establishing as its work other fictions, installing a politics out of its acting.

c) An approach to the rectangular space-format of the stage, disconnected from previous models of construction, allows us to perceive it and relate to it as an abstract place, one that doesn't contain a predetermined ideology or paradigm for constructing a narration. This allows its appearance as a space for creation that permits a re-decontextualization of stage language, opening horizons for the realization of gestures of creation that come from the encounter between the notions already described.

The perspective on theatre creation derived from the premises of The Dramaturgy of Space returns us to situating ourselves in terms of, or to thinking about, initial creative gestures for reconstructing other writings, and brings us to approach performance from basic stage actions derived from the format.

We have established that the human being chose the rectangular format for constructing the poetics of his/her imaginary, developing from it a visual narrative.

The whole process of theatre art can be conceived as the process of generating fictions within the rectangular format from infinite mechanisms of decontextualization. Codes for performance are abstracted: a text, a body, the music, an object, in order to introduce them into the three-dimensional stage space, creating a fiction that is constituted from its spatial (space-time) narrative.

Thus, theatre language in its totality is constructed from its own processes and generates its own autonomous conventions and universes in the face of the constructions of the dimension of reality.

Subscribing to the rectangle as the geometric place for our artistic representations, we have generated a common site for arts that construct themselves on the basis of this format: so that the study of compositional narrative laws has conformed to a transversal language with specific structures for each expression, whether they comprise a two-dimensional or three-dimensional rectangular format.

The flat space of the pictorial arts, its study of the golden mean—golden rectangle—of its tension, proportions, and manipulation of perspectives, horizons, volumes, symmetries, and lines of force, also acquires relevance for graphics, architecture, photographic composition, and, later on, the development of cinematographic narrative, with its planes, frames, and conceptions of montage. Stage art (dance, theatre) is intrinsically connected to this common space: the language of the ephemeral architecture of scenery, or its installations, lighting design, costume design, all originates from the same common concepts.

The *Dramaturgy of Space* constitutes part of this tradition and reconstitutes in its three-dimensionality, and at times in the writing of its texts—written for a rectangular format—the same origin and finality, profoundly differentiating its application in relation to the history of the discipline and in the inherent gestures of performance in each period.

This theoretical conception comes from this origin and difference: as we put its notions into practice, we are searching for a way for us to approach the processes of decontextualization for this profession and a way of initiating an artistic construction.

Within this frame, the proposed exercises that follow help us realize some of the elements of the stage alphabet. They give us an approach to working with the body and the object in space, to explore its impact on the construction of styles and spatial narratives.

They have been abstracted from creative processes in which I have been involved. Derived first from dramatic visual dramaturgies that demand a poetics of space to contain them, or from transforming the foundation for the construction of productions, and as a tool for actor training.

The video links in the text provide audiovisual support and give us an idea of some basic possibilities for application. Each exercise described is only a platform from which to work; they are for those who apply them, amplify them, diversify them, deconstruct them, and develop them on the basis of their own codes for performance.

# The Dissection of the Format

We will undertake a geometric dissection of the stage rectangle which, besides its formality, contains elements of the narrative content. The following application permits us to reveal hidden lines of support and serves us as a basis for the practical work of the stage exercises.

## Platform for Actions

In our rehearsal hall we trace a rectangle with adhesive tape, leaving a passage area around its perimeter. Inside of this we trace the two principal diagonals and then divide it into three equidistant parallel horizontal and three vertical lines; finally, starting from the center, we trace the circle the rectangle contains.

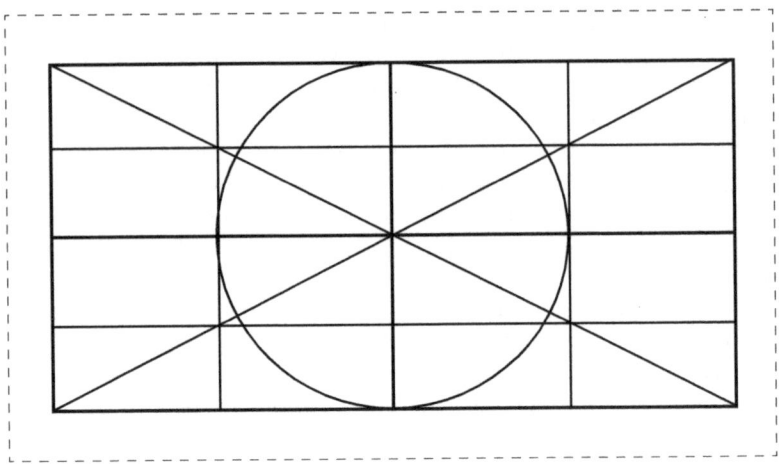

Although this is a schematic planimetrical design, we situate ourselves in three-dimensional space, where these lines and geometric figures are projected in space.

The materialization of the virtual lines reveals to us some of the geometric figures this dissection contains.

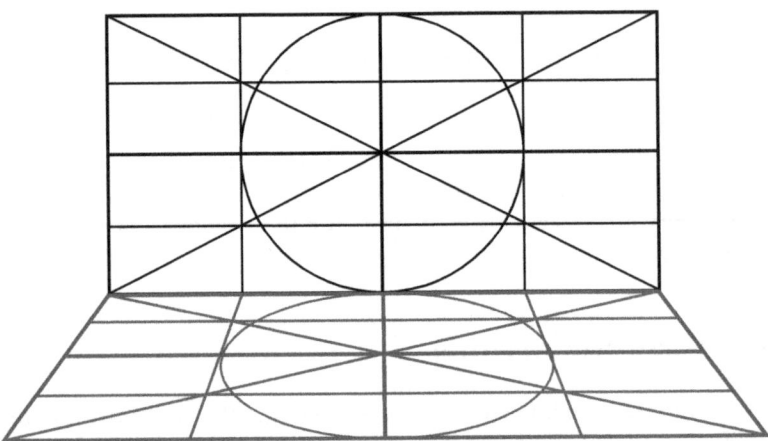

We appreciate how this subdivision generates other rectangles, that can be divided in the same manner an infinite number of times. The rectangular frame, as a container of infinite frames, is the

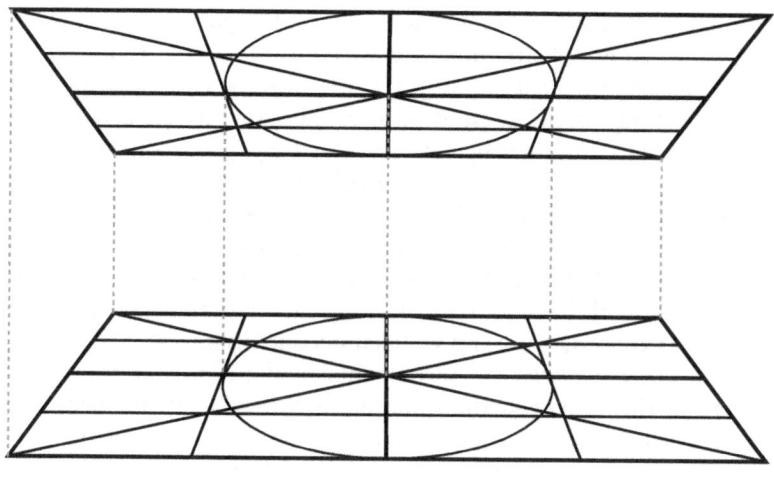

73

abstraction of a visual narrative; this aspect of the format supports spatial-temporal compositions that, as a sum of their sequences, construct the diagram of narrative forms.

# Body and Decontextualization of the Stage Space

## ACTIONS 1
### Individual Organic Compositions

https://griffero.cl/la-dramaturgia-del-espacio/#uael-video-gallery-a40ea18-1

From the center of the space we ask the participants to place themselves around the perimeter, on the lateral lines and at the back, leaving the frontal area free. Then we tell them to individually enter the space from whichever direction they choose and say their name.

Generally, the interpreter will enter the space uncomfortable with the requested situation and without putting into motion the decontextualization of the body. There is no immediate consciousness that the body is being framed, and, therefore, visualized from a different place and that by virtue of this stage process it is revealed as a sign of the species, a performing body.

A series of peripheral movements will appear, defined as those unconscious gestures of body language, finger movements, eyebrows, rocking, that we don't control and that only express discomfort with being onstage. Product of the notion of being seen, of being exposed, of feeling yourself decontextualized.

The clear majority of participants tend to stop in the center, situating themselves in the same place from which the directions were given. It seems that the visual perception of the place of direction is usually more significant than hearing what the word has indicated.

This happens because they apply in the first instance the daily habits of the body on the stage, reiterating them onstage without much reflection: the tendency is that when the interpreter comes onstage to say their name, they won't say it from a corner, but situate themselves in the center, like someone about to receive a diploma or pose for a photograph. We will see a lack of focus in everything including the rhythm of their walk. There is no consciousness of an exposed body, of being unmasked by its actions.

## Directions

We will point out that the body has different axes, not just the frontal one. That the space is constituted by all the planes of the rectangle and that the center is not necessarily its strongest point. The central point of the stage gives force to the acting body, although we will see later that some spatial lines increase narrative tensions and generate more energy centers than others.

**ACTIONS 1B**
**Collective Organic Compositions**

https://griffero.cl/la-dramaturgia-del-espacio/#uael-video-gallery-a40ea18-2

# CHAPTER II

> We ask the participants to enter the space walking at their normal pace, emphasizing how their presence alters the space, with their focus (gaze) straight ahead, avoiding any side gesture that would induce them to underscore other unwanted points of attraction. Upon arriving at the indicated spot, they are to realize an organic composition: once it is configured, they should direct their focus to the spectators and say their name. This may imply a turning of the head or of the torso. Upon leaving, drop the focus, relax the composition, and leave the space.

This exercise puts into action the relationships between the body and the space, making you conscious that this is determined by the frame and the interpolation is underlined by your focus. According to the composition organically assumed by the body an emotional state will always be perceived. The manipulation of the body in relation to the space generates presence and determines the way in which it wants to be seen, read, or signified.

In the previous exercise, we took a small step in the construction of a stage presence, one that will then be strengthened by the text, voice, and emotion. What we traditionally catalog as "stage presence" is the magnetism or aura generated by a body when it is decontextualized. Presence, which could be a response to so-called "charisma," responds to a series of factors that intuition or studying the body onstage put into action. The interpreter, upon adapting the multiple relationships of their body language with the space, upon succeeding in controlling the decontextualization, begins to give weight, mystery, to their state of being, provoking the spectator's gaze to center on their action.

When we come face to face with two actors with the same interpretative level when working on a text, the one that stands out will be the one who develops a use of the dramatic body in space in their interpretation. Let's remember that the body finds itself within a rectangle framed in relation to it, and its compositions and foci give us the form and content of its emotional-narrative state.

In the stage space it is the actor's body that constructs its own frames until it succeeds in transforming itself (analogically)—into the camera's viewfinder that guides the spectator's perception.

These are general principles, which we will break down as we go along in relation to organic, graphic, or conceptual forms of composition and how these interact with different foci, the stage planes, rhythms of displacement, direction, the interrelation between bodies and space, and the association between compositions.

## The Organic Composition (Functional and Intimate)

The organic composition is whichever of the infinite bodily compositions we realize daily, the hundreds of ways we lie down, sit down, stand, etc. In every place, beach, park, classroom, library, finally... there will be hundreds of possible organic compositions each one different from the other.

A composition isn't a frozen action, it is a *state of being*, it reflects an interior state: upon extending our body on the stage, we become conscious of the distribution of our feet, head, hands, and the direction of our gaze.

Organic compositions are infinite and vary according to the place and situation in which the body finds itself and its pervading state of being.

When the corporeal disposition adjusts itself in relation to the public space where it is inserted, following the norms and "correct" habits of a social body, the compositions have a functional character.

In our intimacy the organic compositions acquire other figures, either in relation to themselves or others and according to the emotions they summon. When the body reflects intimate states of being: emotions, love, happiness, rage, deception, or challenging situations: abandonment, solitude, hope. In a forest, a hotel room, or a bathtub, the body, disconnected from its social presence, amplifies the gamut of its compositions, upon being liberated from the cultural context—the public one—that conditions it.

In decontextualization exercises these compositions are fundamental since they amplify the register of figures that the body can construct, and, therefore, give us a greater recognition of our visual-emotive states of being.

Intimate composition gives more planes to the bodily state, reflecting its internal world, a basic question of dramatic art. At the same time the stage space can contain, in the same frame, both functional and intimate compositions, generating their own associations on the stage. All of this is proposed from an abstraction, where predetermined emotions haven't yet entered into play. Upon executing these first approaches, keep in mind that each one of these basic actions has as its objective to realize a stage truth at its fundamentals and its development is, therefore, unlimited, as infinite as creation.

We are working in the empty space, without objects, furniture, or scenic installations. Their later incorporation will allow us to reconstitute and amplify the gamut of corporeal compositions.

## ACTIONS 2
### Organic Compositions in Sequence

https://griffero.cl/la-dramaturgia-del-espacio/#uael-video-gallery-a40ea18-3

*Each exercise can be done with two people in the space and then add participants (2, 6, 12, etc.) in relation to the dimensions of the working area.*

A performer enters the space, stops at the place they choose, and realizes an organic composition. Then a second person repeats the gesture, and each succeeding person does the same. As the final participant finishes, everyone turns their focus on the audience, then they relax in unison and leave.

Let's see how we've produced a body–space order, facilitating the spectator's perception of the compositions.

　　a) We repeat the previous exercise, this time after the entrance of the last participant. The first person, without leaving the area, moves to another place on the stage and realizes another composition and everyone follows in succession; the whole group makes a sequence of compositional frames.

b) The previous exercise is repeated, with the variation that after the entrance of the last participant, everyone moves in unison to the second composition, then the third, fourth, etc.

c) Now the entrances into the space can be realized with variations in time between them, in pairs, or with the entire group in unison... The second movements can vary in time. In the same way, the group won't all leave at once leaving isolated or solitary compositions at the end of the exercise. The idea is to begin to relate entrances and movements to the rhythm with which they are established.

d) The change in compositions in the last exercise doesn't necessarily imply a displacement but can also be executed by means of a change in the composition of the location. The sum of the individual compositions generates for us the general frame, that denotes the beginning of a stage atmosphere, generated by the sum of said compositions.

The previous exercises must develop a consciousness of the dialogue created between the different compositions, in relation to the location and corporeality of the other participants as well as in relation to the spatial distribution.

The compositions of these exercises are not meant to illustrate places. The lines of the space are references for the performer to their location in the different spatial planes (distance–axis–relationship to others), they aren't guides for shifting them.

We can point out in the previous compositions that the direction of our focus (gaze) changes the perception of the spatial/corporeal state, changing the internal narrative and, therefore, guiding and interpolating the spectator from their spatial situation, according to the interpreter's directorial focus.

# Points of Focus in the Stage Space

The movement of our skull, as part of our physiology, determines the place to which we direct our gaze.

If the movement of our ocular globe enables us to change the direction of our gaze, the same variation is applicable in the space of intimate performance. The action of specifying the gaze, realized in the decontextualized space on the stage, constitutes a fundamental element of the spatial narrative and the stage presence of the actor.

Within this grammar of the body–space relationship what I define as focus is not only the place where the actor directs their gaze, but also where we want the spectator to structure their points of attention, which is determined by the composition of the stage. What I want to underline as an actor, interpolating or not interpolating, is the relationship that appears as a result of different reactions to the gaze and the corporeal and focal grammar constructed.

For example, upon proposing foci towards infinity you'd configure essential elements of the space–body grammar that allow us to configure and perceive dialogue structures that the body realizes on and with the space.

The way we read the organic composition of a body is modified by the direction of its focus. A body standing on the stage looking at the audience, or at its hand, or towards the back of the stage, undoubtedly marks for us different intentions and states for this body.

At the same time the foci in the space gain potency from the directions constituted by the geometric diagram of the stage and from the emotive content of the gaze. If all the performers maintain the same focus towards the same direction, they generate points of narrative tension (spatial accents) putting pressure on the dramatic space at the same time as they order the general composition.

### ACTIONS 3
### Cardinal Focus Points

https://griffero.cl/la-dramaturgia-del-espacio/#uael-video-gallery-a40ea18-4

## ACTIONS 3B
## Multiple Focus Points

https://griffero.cl/la-dramaturgia-del-espacio/#uael-video-gallery-a40ea18-5

All the participants enter the work area. We indicate five cardinal points of focus in the space: to the back, the left, the right, the ground, and the front. The interpreters disperse themselves rapidly in the space, stop in unison, and direct their gaze at the first point indicated, disperse themselves and stop, focusing on the second point, and so forth.

We can see that the space, perceived in the first instance in chaotic form, automatically becomes organized when the bodies stop and direct their gaze at a determined point, generating a spatial order and a point of tension.

Variations:

a) With the last movement proceed to generate three successive cardinal points of focus, all from the place you landed with the last movement.

b) Half the interpreters define a focal direction distinct from that chosen by the other half.

c) At normal rhythm and with different entrances each participant defines their focus using different cardinal points; develop various sequences.

The interpreter enters the space walking at a normal pace, this can be done individually or in pairs, and chooses a focus, then the second, third, etc. enters. When the first sequence is finished, they disperse without leaving the space and upon arriving at another location generate another focus.

In these first exercises with focal points we only work with the body in its vertical position that is only displaced and situated in the space in relation to its own coordinates and those of others. This is done to isolate and perceive the effect of the virtual and linear directions of focus from the geometry of the space. In this instance, the relation body/space/rhythm/time is associated with the basic principles of dance.

## The Use of Focus for Organization in Large Spaces, and with Big Groups

The focal technique is a primordial element in the organization of numerous groups in wide-open spaces. Choreography in a stadium, for example, organizes itself automatically when you indicate to five hundred people that they should disperse focusing on the scoreboard and, once they get to the center, they should focus on the ground indefinitely.

In an opera the chorus advances singing, focusing on a character, then they unsheathe their swords, raise them, and focus upon them, thus choreographing their displacement, maintaining an order and a scenic reading. In the same fashion military parades, processions, or gymnastic groups organize themselves in relation to predetermined points of focus and gestures.

The fictional focal point is an element of the grammar of the language of the stage, since in real life we don't walk around focusing on our hands, nor do we enter a room focusing on the sky.

By organizing the body and the focal point in the space we produce fictional moments that in the first instance call our attention to the perception of a state or atmosphere, interpolating the spectator, guiding their gaze, and with it, their senses and feelings.

## Typology of Focal Points in the Stage Space

The following nomenclature defines for us a variety of stage focal points and the narrative ascribed to them.

### *Focal Points Beyond the Limits of the Stage*

Every focal point that is directed beyond the stage space conveys us towards a fictional place; the space the actor visualizes in this beyond. This beyond can be a concrete place of visualization, like the external gaze of a mental image.

From the stage, we visualize beyond its limits: a boat pulling away, birds flying on the horizon, a battlefield, an advancing army, the city and its lights, the infinity of the universe, visions of gods or demons, the metaphysics of the abstract void, or our emotional states.

The external focal point creates an emotional echo of the interpreter's visualization. At the same time, it allows the projection of a present, past, or future state. This focal point in the spatial narrative is a crucial element of fiction since the stage, due to its physical dimension, can't contain the universe of places that we represent or suggest.

The actor situated in a fictional stadium, by means of their external focal point (linked to their corporeal-physical gesture) gives imaginary presence to the entire audience, observing from the stadium, widening the narrative space independently of the architectonic delimitation of the rectangle.

The stage space as a support for a fiction has no walls that limit it, but it has horizons and the sky. The focal point is what broadens the limits of the rectangle, revealing all that is situated on the virtual horizon of fiction. A scenographic construction or installation will give spatial delimitations to the fiction it wants to represent, always leaving free the horizon situated behind the spectator.

Thus, the external focus projects and amplifies the place of its fiction, as well as the state of its spirit, since this gaze isn't only a linear direction but also the visualization of what it perceives beyond.

## *Focus on the Audience*

The focus on the audience is one that directly interpolates the spectator, that acknowledges them in their space and as to whom the text is directed. In classical dramaturgy we have the so-called "aside," which is signaled by the playwright as an interpolation in the narrative. A recourse utilized in some dramatic structures, or productions, to break the fiction of character or of a situation, or, in the Brechtian theatre, as a distancing effect.

The focus on the audience in stage spectacles is inherent to this element, since one doesn't speak from the stage space as if it were a fictional place, but from the stage in terms of what it supports (dramatic readings, comedy shows, musicals).

We also have the monologue-dialogue to the audience, or the genre of monodrama where, in some dramatic structures, the pre-established interlocutor is the spectator.

## *A Variant on the Content of the Focus on the Audience: The Performative Focus*

The focus or direction of the gaze also plays a "performative" role where the content or the actor's dialogue with the audience generates a relationship, not as someone who interpolates from a fiction, but from a place of auto-representation, situating themselves in the same present and from the same ambience as those who are watching. This focus tends to cancel the effect of speaking from another temporal fiction and wants to eliminate the separation between actor and spectator. In any case, another type of convention is established, since whoever talks from a performative space is situated in a place of decontextualized actions.

For example, in a dramatic situation of "put in the abyss" in *Fin de Eclipse*, the actor stops the action and interpolates the spectator saying, "I don't know what to say, I've never lived this, I don't know how to act it."

## *Focal Points of Dialogue Towards the Interior of the Stage Space*

This focal point is developed in the interior of the rectangular space and doesn't project beyond its limits. It is defined as a focal point of internal dialogue, since its action refers us to a situation of dialogue. Although we should point out that all the typologies of focus imply the determination and perception of a dialogue.

An interpreter in the space, upon directing their gaze towards the body of another interpreter or towards an object, establishes a dialogue. If this is developed in its space-time sequences, the succession of focal points in the interior of the space constructs a narration.

Let's imagine the following sequence between a man and a woman: he focuses on her body, she looks at the ground, he focuses on the ground, she looks at him, he looks at her/his feet, they both focus on the horizon.

If a body is alone inside the rectangle and its focus is directed towards different points of this geometry, we perceive the individual's internal dialogue with the space-place. This determination doesn't imply that to establish a stage dialogue between two actors it is necessary to interpolate another looking at them. Sometimes the actions, the text, or the spatial compositions are what establishes the dialogue.

## *Focus on the Body*

This is the gaze that centers on a part of our physiognomy, directing itself towards our clothing, or on the uncovered parts of our body. For example, the interpreter raises their hand and directs their focus towards it, increasing the value of the gesture, like "zooming in" on that extremity.

## *Internal Focus or Interior Gaze*

This focal point is one that connotes the state of a body that isn't in the physical present, but in the temporality of its thought—an "id" focus—but concentrated, like a focus on an internal state.

This focal point transmits a sensation of being suspended to the body. This enables the spectator to approach the subjective dimension of the interpreter. In order to perceive it, let's put our finger on the back of our skull and let's concentrate on that point: we will achieve the sensation of an internal gaze. This happens organically when our thoughts abstract us from our surroundings.

## *Continuous Focal Points*

This is what we call it when the movement of the skull is directed towards different places on the stage, at the actor's body or at others, or in a continuous manner, marking the directions with the axes of the head, or fragmenting the directions, and in this way generating diverse rhythms.

## *Panning Focus*

This is the displacement of the skull—and, therefore, the gaze—like the panning of a camera.

Utilizing the typology of focal points described let's develop the following actions:

> ## ACTIONS 4
> ## Organic Compositions and Focus Points
> https://griffero.cl/la-dramaturgia-del-espacio/#uael-video-gallery-a40ea18-6
>
> a) In the first sequence all the participants, in vertical composition, apply external focus. In the second sequence the focal point is on oneself (without leaving the space). In the third sequence the focal point is the dialogue. In the fourth sequence the focal point is internal. In the fifth sequence the focal point is the audience.
>
> Develop variants of the exercise in the desired number of sequences and the alternating use of the typologies described.
>
> b) Organic compositions and their focal points:
>
> Consciousness of all the relationships and the global composition of the frames. As the exercise is realized, let's contemplate the disposition and displacement of bodies in relation to the diverse organic compositions, focal points, and spatial distributions.
>
> c) Choose an aural or musical theme, which will help give us rhythm and atmosphere (literal or subjective). Utilize the typology of focal points in the desired order. The participants' focal points can be worked on in unison, in partial form, or individually. One group works on one type, another with another and alternating, according to the development of the work.
>
> Note how, although departing from an abstract exercise, the sum of the frames realized already narrate themselves without a predetermined direction. One variant of this exercise consists of preparing a combination of frames upon which we seek to imprint a predetermined atmosphere.

# Focal Points: Composition and Content

They say that the gaze is "the mirror of the soul." Let's say that it possesses and carries an emotional content that can indicate conflict or internal peace. The gaze talks to us. So that, in principle, a neutral gaze never existed, since it is a sign of the person making it.

The person who looks, hears, judges, feels; he who sees, depending upon what he looks at, sees what he judges, or feels, and this is reflected in him or her at the same time. Therefore, our neutral gaze already carries a content, that we carry or underline when we give it the emotion and feelings we perform.

This action realized in the decontextualized space of the stage constitutes a fundamental element of the spatial narrative and of the stage presence of the actor. A focal point, by underlining the direction of the gaze, generates an accent and an interpolation and organizes the narrative geometry of the space.

> **ACTIONS 4B**
> **Dialogue Focus Points. Internal Focus Points With Oneself**
>
> https://griffero.cl/la-dramaturgia-del-espacio/#uael-video-gallery-a40ea18-7
>
> With an aural-musical background, which gives rhythm and atmosphere to the exercise, let's produce corporeal compositions in each sequence ascribing to them a pre-established emotive state.

> **ACTIONS 4C**
> **Typology of Focus Points and Atmosphere**
>
> https://griffero.cl/la-dramaturgia-del-espacio/#uael-video-gallery-a40ea18-8
>
> Variant: frame sequence, each performer links their desired emotion to their composition and focal point.

# Graphic Corporeal Composition

Despite the infinite compositions a body can realize, they can be organized into two axes or lines of construction, an organic one—to which we have already referred—and a graphic one.

The graphic composition of the body in daily life has been associated with the signification of political, religious, sporting, and military ritual. Given that the abstraction of a graphic gesture and its corporeal reproduction imply the body's adhesion to a predetermined and conscious sign, it is not an organic gesture.

We know why we raise our left fist, or salute militarily raising the hand to the forehead. By the same token, we put our hands together to pray, a priest blesses with the sign of the cross, we put our hand on our heart, or raise our arms in surrender.

Placed in their social scheme bodily graphics carry with them the destructuring of our organic selves, underscoring an emotional or ritual content by means of body language associated with a sign.

So that also in terms of stage fiction, the corporeal elaboration of graphic signs causes us to construct subtextual significations and to invent our own graphics for our corporeal story. The graphics of the actorly body don't simply refer to the formal graphics of the gymnasium, but to the underlying emotive, abstract, and metaphysical content.

In this form of composition, the body presents itself as a graphic, geometrical element, installing an action and a signification. The *Vitruvian Man*, the classic da Vinci drawing, is the image of a graphic composition, the body as a cross. The graphic composition brings us to the conventions of the abstract body, where its lines, and angles in relation to the lines, and the angles of the space, form a whole.

Onstage the actor's role is to give each graphic composition a content and an emotion, establishing a distinctive corporeal sign. The graphic in these exercises isn't considered from the point of view of mime or corporeal illustration.

The graphic composition arises out of the organic composition and returns to it, establishing by its action and displacement markers in the action.

> **ACTIONS 5**
> **Graphic Corporeal Composition**
>
> https://griffero.cl/la-dramaturgia-del-espacio/#uael-video-gallery-a40ea18-9
> Organic compositions and corporeal graphics
>
> *Graphic compositions*
> The participants enter the working area one by one; they propose diverse graphic compositions in relation to the focal points and the space, realizing three that alter the space and three that conform to it. Then the participants establish among others, a graphic gestural choreography (sequence, displacements, interspersed, in the place, together) in relation to the atmosphere and rhythm given by a musical composition.
>
> *Organic and graphic composition*
> The exercise intersperses the alternating use of two compositions.

In this stage composition let's first establish the organic composition from which the graphic composition emerges. It then falls apart and an organic composition is taken up again. Let's realize several sequences without leaving the stage. At the end of the sequence three, two, or one interpreters are left.

Our displacement can establish itself without dissolving the composition. For example, I advance with hands outstretched and my focus on them and towards the front.

In order to avoid the sensation of a photographic sequence—one image, displacement, second image—let's remember that the compositions can vary from the same place, or that having displaced ourselves, the direction of the focal point doesn't necessarily follow the axis of the body.

# Organic-Graphic Composition and Costuming

Our clothes are certainly a determining sign in signaling who or what we represent. Clothing signals social strata, hierarchy, psychological personality, cultural level, and style. It reflects the emotional state and condition of the interpreter, eras, textures, volumes, color, and innumerable other metaphorical-psychological-social characteristics.

These exercises will change their meaning and capacity for interpolation, depending upon what the interpreters wear. What interests us in this section is that in organic or graphic corporeal compositions the clothing that appears on the stage can be considered another element in the development of bodily compositions.

The ways in which we appropriate pieces of clothing and how we manipulate them incite and influence our perception of states of being, and the dialogues and situations that we suggest through the image.

At the same time the composition interacting with the piece of clothing will point out the covered and uncovered parts of our body, fragmenting in its sequence the naked places, generating bodily graphics by means of kinesthetic movement. For example, we lift our undershirt, revealing our torso, and covering our face.

The actions of the previous exercises, presented as a sequence of naked bodies, would also create a narrative based on the abstraction of the human body in a space. That brings us to a reading of the contents that those bodies manifest, referring us to new places and atmospheres. Since we are developing in this book the previous or subtextual language of narrative space, we are interested in underlining this.

## ACTIONS 6
## Graphic Composition, Organic and Costume Design

https://griffero.cl/la-dramaturgia-del-espacio/#uael-video-gallery-a40ea18-10

Organic and graphic compositions in relation to the clothing of the participants.

a) Uniformity of clothing: men in formal dress, women in long dresses. All in sportswear, all in winter clothing, all in institutional uniforms, all in underwear, all in clothing from a particular period (the 1960s, the 1970s), or social class, or youth subculture, etc.

b) Diversity of clothing/costuming on the stage and in compositions, search for spontaneous spatial narrations based on the combinations that arise: one performer as a nurse, another as a motorcyclist, a third with boxing gloves, someone in jeans with a naked torso, etc.

c) Exchanging clothing between the participants, restructuring the stage signs with the reappropriated clothing: four interpreters realize the first sequences, then they dispose of their clothing on the stage and appropriate that of any one of the other participants.

If these examples are random, by introducing costuming in the exercises, whether in uniformity or diversity, we construct atmosphere, concepts, narrations, that produce for us a gamut of associations by imprinting on the actors' bodies identifying icons that generate a multiplicity of perceptions, dialogues, and feelings, in accord with the chosen clothing.

The intention of the exercise isn't to delve deeply into the foregoing, since we would then be entering the sphere of constructing fictions in relation to a production, which would lead us to cover the concepts of costume design—a theatrical text or language of its own—that is an inherent part of the poetics of the spatial dramaturgy.

# The Body and Geometric Narrative of the Format

We have pointed out some concepts that define composition in relation to the sketch of the body and its focal points. To deepen this narrative it is fundamental to create a clear sense of our corporeal drawing in dialogue with the geometry of the stage, its planes and diagonals.

The boundaries of our rectangle confine what is within and without the field of action, as well as forming a temporal space that generates the convention for the beginning or the end of situations, upon entering or exiting them. Given that several rectangles exist within the macro rectangle of the stage, the narrative rectangle allows us to read beginnings and endings within each one of them.

In the design of the rectangular space, we tend to associate the right vertex with positive points and the left vertex with negative.

Based on this reading, displacements from the left to the right are seen to give a positive weight to the action: triumph, happiness, etc., while those from the right to the left acquire a more dramatic weight. Thus, traditionally, a cinematic take of an attacking army carries more force if it is filmed from the left towards the right of the rectangle screen, and the return of the vanquished is more pathetic if the take is from the right to the left, while the diagonal lines of the perspective give us the points of flight.

In the old theatre of the star system on the Italianate stage the leading actor "took the stage"—that's to say, entered—from the positive point displacing himself on the diagonal until reaching the center, creating a playing space in the triangle of the first plane of the stage.

In this traditional concept of theatricality, the actor's entrance, from the diagonal of the positive point of the stage, implied a greater protagonist and his exit utilized the right point. Thus, for scenic equilibrium, the antagonist made his appearance from the negative point. When the interpreter situates themselves in whichever of these points, they succeed in directing the spectators' focus towards the same point.

If we situate ourselves from the point of view of the spectator, the implication is that all focal points are oriented in the direction, if it is the right side, positive, it will evoke the idea of the beginning of the reading.

Upon situating themselves in the center the actor brings it about that a third of house left watches from the left flank, those in the center from the front, and the other third from the right flank, joining the sightlines in the stage triangle, permitting or facilitating a concentration of energy on that point. At the same time, the so-called "three-quarters" position of the body facilitates bodily movement on its axis, interpolating itself towards the different places of the house without needing to displace itself, in the same way as when it directs itself towards the interpreters that are on different planes of the stage.

The utilization of the format's geometry is inherent to all the historic gestures of scenic composition, and in the intent to create the convention of a representation. The lines of the rectangular space join the bodies together on the stage establishing tensions and dialogues.

Next, we will point out the most notable aspects.

## *Diagonals*

The greatest lines of tension are those that are projected when bodies are situated on the diagonal trajectory. Two interpreters situated on the same diagonal give the sensation of greater spatial tension to this relation, or to the situation described: a threat, an encounter, a goodbye, a duel. At the same time, they are lines that have a greater sense of escape. Consider them lines of force in the space.

## *Triangles and Pyramidal Compositions*

Diagonals trace triangles on the interior of the space, allowing visual composition of triangles or pyramidales, generating points of tension projected at the interior or exterior of the space. In the composition "tip of the spear" we organize into a hierarchy the actor's presence according to placement, planes, and axes of the actors. The simultaneous presentation of pyramidal compositions produces multiple tensions, when we position the bodies in diverse interlineal relationships where they have to cross each other or intersect.

## *Horizontals*

Bodies on the horizontal lines tend towards harmony, balance, tranquility, repose: a body lying down on the horizontal accentuates states of sleep, death, sensuality. Three vertical bodies lined up on the horizontal at the back of the stage give us the sense of a stopped action, but since those lines are on an axis with the vertical ones (of the plane), they result in a sensation of beginning, of an action that is going to succeed.

The horizontal, certainly, gives us the concept of the horizon. Horizontals at the same time divide the planes of depth on the stage, creating perceptions of deep fields and multiple horizons.

In dance we appreciate many times, the "sweeps"—bodies that enter from different horizontals—crossing the rectangle, creating the sensation of spatial melting.

## *Verticals*

They are intermediate lines of tension between the effects of diagonal and horizontal lines. These lines create two points of tension in relation to the body's axis and its presence in front of the spectator. A body's frontal approach from upstage to downstage, or its inverse retreat, distancing the back, analogically creates a "zoom" effect, since the body, displaced on the vertical, crosses the different spatial and temporal planes of the scene.

Since they take place within a tridimensional space, surveying the pattern of these exercises doesn't reveal the weight of the lines that are projected upward in the space, where the vertical produces multiple axes of strength and stability, and makes us perceive the variation of bodies in relation to their equilibrium or points of gravity. We can characterize the vertical as a direction in planimetry and an axis in its tridimensionality.

The different readings in relation to the lines of the space will vary according to the direction of the corporeal axis, its focal point and the distance traveled. A body displaced on the vertical with its focal point towards the horizontal makes the different virtual lines of the space converge.

Crossing the stage on a horizontal with a focal point in relation to its axis, you will diversify the geometric-body relationships. We are referring to abstract tensions, those that will later acquire force and be transformed by the text-emotion, situation-illumination, sound and scenic language where they are inserted.

## *The Circle*

The circle evokes stability, harmony, concordance, and respect. Even though it covers the area of the entire rectangle, given our rectangular construction it won't often be dominant in the construction of narratives. In any case, its capacity for the infinite has created stage machinery that allows spatial and temporal changes, such as the revolve. Bodies in a circle establish balance in relation to the axes of the geometric figure and for this to continue being visualized, they must maintain equidistance from the center. When we create the appearance of balance breaking it creates narrative tension. The circular carries with it an internal infinite, it is not a line that projects itself like a vertical or a diagonal beyond the scene. The axis of the circle corresponds to the center of the rectangle.

Turning the body on its own axis constitutes the minimal relationship of the body with the circle in the scene. And circular displacement gives the perception of a spiral or of centrifugal movements. The difficulty of its narrative lies in the fact that it has no beginning and no end, it doesn't imply an entrance or an exit from the rectangle.

## Symmetry and Asymmetry

The visual narratives produced in the space will be constituted by symmetrical or asymmetrical relationships. Consciously or unconsciously, the external gaze, as much as internal perception, will move in relation to these two variables in staging.

As a complement to the concepts of symmetry and asymmetry in the stage space, we talk about imbalance when an area of the stage carries more weight in the distribution of bodies than another area.

The performers will proceed to look for spatial equilibrium, by means of a uniform distribution, an effect of balanced equilibrium.

One must point out that a traditionally balanced space isn't always a condition for a successful spatial work. Where the perception of visual equilibrium isn't necessarily ruled by this proceeding, but by dramatic actions, textual poetics and the performers' scenic presence form the balance as much as the geometrical spatial distribution.

If we have three performers on the upstage left vertex and another performer in the contrary area, our dramatic focal point will be on the solitary performer. In this example asymmetrical balance gives force to the scene. But with whichever subsequent movement the scene will be strengthened by the symmetry generated, establishing a metaphysical-dialectical relationship.

Each scenic creation will discover where the perception of the scene, or of the sequences, or of the staging, centers on a symmetrical or asymmetrical vision, or on the preponderance in the play between them, and will intervene in its time besides the body, volumes, objects, movements of stage machinery, lighting or audiovisual resources that appear, thus modifying the relationship between these two variables.

## Symmetry–Asymmetry in Corporeal Composition

The body is a geometric structure, limited by its physiology in terms of the variations it can generate in its compositions by asymmetry and symmetry.

Social behavior induces a symmetrical composition of our body, that upon seeing itself put in order, becomes a reflection of the social order. The more disciplined the social institution, the more symmetrical the corporeal compositions demanded: armed forces, security forces, judiciary, churches, educational centers, businesses, of political power, etc.

We can confirm that in the codes of rebellion of juvenile groups destructuring of corporeal symmetry is assimilated as a gesture of identitary autonomy or anti-systemic attitude. At the same time, asymmetrical compositions are socialized in spaces of social diversion: beaches, nocturnal centers, personal spaces. In the scenic space these compositions are inherent to the structure of theatrical language, where we delve into the kinetic symmetries and asymmetries of the body, and we invent our own compositions for the scene.

There are three levels to consider in these compositions: our symmetrical and asymmetrical relationship to the space, our relationship to our own body, and our relationship to the other performers.

In relation to the areas of the rectangular stage, let's remember that our workspace is itself configured into sixteen sub rectangles each one of which contains in itself all of the geometric figures, whether seen as unified or as a grouping of the internal rectangular areas: the division into two rectangular areas left–right, or into four areas, two upstage, two downstage, etc.

What's important here isn't so much the imposition of formal structures for analysis, as understanding the possibilities they open up. The ability to award each area a different temporal space, allowing the coexistence of simultaneous and alternating parallel universes and scenic fictions within the general rectangle.

At the same time the positive, negative, diagonal, horizontal, and other geometric distinctions exist in the interior of each rectangle contained in the general frame. From which springs the infinite possibilities of the visual narrative.

## ACTIONS 7
## Asymmetry: Body–Space Lines and Tensions, Body–Space Geometry, Body–Space Circular and Triangular Geometry, Body–Space Symmetry and Asymmetry

https://griffero.cl/la-dramaturgia-del-espacio/#uael-video-gallery-a40ea18-11

a) Prepare, with the support of a musical structure, a spatial scheme where, by means of an almost choreographic progression, compositions and displacements are interwoven and built in the space, in relation to a combination of formal lines and subdivision of the areas.

b) Compositions with vertical-organic or graphic body, displacements with respect to the diagonals, then horizontals and verticals, creating a spatial choreography.

c) Compositions using the triangular or circular in the space.

d) Compositions underlining bodily symmetrical and asymmetrical balance and symmetrical and asymmetrical spatial balance.

*Variations*
In the development of the exercise, all the performers, whether in the same areas or distributed, can construct some corporeal

> compositions identical to those of the other performers, as in a game of mirrors.
>
> Example: Four performers enter from upstage, they stop, creating the same composition, they displace themselves in different directions, they sit down in the same way, with the same axis, etc.
>
> The variations of this bodily symmetry mirror one another. The spatial distribution is different but the bodily compositions is identical.
>
> Variation: Within the interior of the symmetrical and asymmetrical sequences, establish movements of identical bodily symmetry.

We deduce that in the dynamics of the compositions various planes interact, simultaneously. The application of these actions doesn't imply populating the space to its full extent. Let's consider: emptinesses, distances, tensions, and groups.

When composing in the space we have the unconscious tendency to give the space a concrete location beforehand, not an abstract one, and to construct fictions that denote a reflection of situations in accord with our habitual use of spaces (everyone around a bonfire, in a room, in a church, at a train stop, on the beach.) Compositions in relation to the space and the position of the other within it should tend to create figures that don't illustrate quotidian situations.

When we represent a place, we can also construct an abstraction of that illustration, utilizing the coordinates of the spatial geometry and not necessarily in relation to the geometry of reality. Scenic language constructs its own situations of spatial dialogue and of representation of fictional places. For example, in "reality" we don't speak to someone when our bodies are back-to-back and situated on the horizontal.

The convention of scenic language allows the deconstruction of the social geometry of daily relations, giving them other structures that derive from the empty space and that will never exist as such in our surroundings. Onstage we produce the decontextualization of a situation and not implicitly the compositional conditions for it to refer to reality.

The development of these exercises, which brings us closer to an intimate relationship with the space and allows us to construct our own scenic creations, comes from there. Having first established a relationship of bodies with their geometry and with that of the scenic space, we invent other emotional and sensorial relationships, attributing to our relationship with the space an affective connotation, allowing a corporeal language to emerge, which belongs to the scene, which reveals states and emotions to us on the basis of other illustrations, constructing a spatial narrative with our body, giving an appropriation and a definition, to a narrative that makes us travel to other corners or representations of our states of being.

## Of the Actorly Body in the Space: The Poetics of the Body

The body in the scenic space isn't our everyday body, the one we represent, but a scenic one. This doesn't imply that an actor has to have certain predetermined physical characteristics, but that they should be capable of transforming themselves in an iconic emotive gesture.

It isn't relevant that an interpreter walks in a disarticulated manner in their daily life, or stands up straight, is overweight, is timid, or speaks slowly, as long as we find ourselves in front of a body whose own condition reflects a history and a personality. It isn't in the interest of art to change personalities that have been constructed from a social context.

But it is essential that the actor on the stage can re-interpret themselves, modify themselves, produce appropriate kinesics and states of being, interpreting bodies that aren't their gender, age, or condition, and successfully incarnate a sick, psychotic, aggressive, sensual, timid body, or a body from a particular time period or of a dramatic symbology or archetype (time, the universe, the atom, the mind).

An actor's objective in their work is to break down the body and make it actorial, be a creator of corporeal fictions in the same way as when they interpret emotions that don't correspond to their own manner of showing them and discover the mechanisms that come into play in this ludic spirit of making the body act.

## CHAPTER II

In this context, physical training doesn't help the interpretation if such training is seen only as form and forgets that the actorial body is form and content at the same time, and that its training should strive to give the actor the tools with which to convey their decontextualization and become fictional.

When we talk about the body in the scenic space for these exercises, we are referring to it before it constitutes a dramatic persona. We are only talking about its characteristics and movements within the representational rectangle, even though the simple presence of a body on the stage constitutes a character for the spectator, in spite of the fact that it isn't representing anything more than itself as a sign.

Given that it is in the scenic space, its clothing, corporeality, or gaze establish the beginning of the convention of a fiction.

Upon coming face to face with a body in the scenic space looking towards the infinite we will perceive it as the beginning of a work, the scenic body becomes an actor, beyond the intention of the performer.

The body in the space is a plastic figure, evocative, a container of emotions. It refers us to situations and generates by its being and movement internal and external actions.

It is a framed figure, abstracted from its surroundings, in front of which we can linger, observe, investigate. In the same way that we can delight ourselves for minutes in the presence of a sculpture, the actorial composition in the space produces in the spectator the visualization of their own body. Their body seen from the point of view of desire, of rejection, of the age and time that it represents.

The body as spirit, as material, as incarnation of the species.

The body onstage provokes, seduces. It is life incarnated and also the place of death, of passions, of horror, of authority, of love.

An interpreter's possible tendency is to be nothing more than a mouthpiece for the word, a word separated from the body, a word that emerges from the vocal cords and the intentions carried by those words, where the body illustrates what the words indicate, like a functional social echo of what is spoken, without using the body as the other text of a text. The actor must be cognizant of the fact that each phrase is a phrase of the body, each idea is an idea incarnated by the body, and each emotion exists within it.

The situation dwells in the actor's body. Dialogue and emotion will be modified by the body's state before the voice enunciates them. Their creation consists of making the body act in relation to the text interpreted, to its silences and to the endless number of images that run through its mind.

Its creation is also to generate gestures that don't necessarily correspond to the formal or cultural illustration conveyed by the text. To say: "How are you?" or "I love you" implies an infinite variety of corporeal versions.

A body that represents subject matter is imbued with compositions that talk to us about the situation and the emotion that are modifying that body. We can perceive what is happening within it in accord with how it is constructed. Its emotions and its spatial temporal relationship will construct a corporeal narrative.

We distinguish a sad body from an erotic body, from a sensual body, from a sick body, from a tortured body; a body that reflects power, a luminous body, or a neurotic body. The actor is the one who constructs the narrative of this body, realizing it through the different states that must be represented.

But since we are in the area of art, where the decontextualization or the reinterpretation of our imaginary also enters into play, the representation of a sick or tortured body isn't necessarily the everyday reference or cliché that we have for that state of being.

The process of creation deconstructs signs, turns them into abstractions, symbolic, conceptual, hyperreal. Spatial-corporeal acting takes us into the infinite world of creation, of the manifestation of subtext, of the literal text, or of its contraction. The body as text, gestures as subtext. Or vice versa.

In corporeal composition subtext allows us to create other signs, that reflect internal states, that become visible. Subtexts exist that are constructions of the soul reflected in the body, determined by an artistic gesture and that don't derive from subtexts of cultural expressions, but from the language of the scene.

The body interpolates, calls, communicates, creates sensations, conveying the spectator by means of the energy of its actions. An actor will develop different mechanisms for interpolating, but scenic creators also bring their own actorial codes for constructing this interpolation.

These acting exercises have as their intention to perceive and present the body in the space for corporeal acting, constructing narrative relationships with the space and transmitting from it, this other dimension, a corporeal grammar that manifests an option that can be perceived by whoever observes it. The aim is that a performer keeps in mind how the narrative is modified from the interior of the space, according to their action, their position, spatial composition, their relationship with the other participants and the general scenic sketch that is constructed, while managing the reading of the global frame from the interior of the space.

A photographer or filmmaker constructs their frames through the rectangle of their viewfinder, registering the composition and the fragment, determining and constructing their narrative as the sum of those frames. In the scenic space the body is its own camera, moving through planes, selecting its frames and managing the rectangular narrative structure, determining external perception.

Upon distinguishing some aspects of our corporeal grammar and its functionality within the space, we will open up other perspectives to associate the body with the text and give its fiction diverse approximations in its scenic construction. It's a matter of visualizing the body-space-time as strung together with the space time of the text and succeeding in constructing body-text-emotion choreography, to develop a fraction of the spatial poetics that, in symbiosis with the textual poetics, will construct the narrative of the work.

# A Story Passes through the Story of the Body-Space it Represents

The stage space divided into planes, segments, lines, tensions, symmetries, and asymmetries constitutes a subliminal narrative that constructs scenic situations, dialogues, and their oppositions.

Begin an autonomous dramatic construction. Autonomous in that beyond our intentions, solely by the composition of bodies and their evolution in the space, do we perceive a narration. Thus, this is basic language for all dramatic composition.

# ACTIONS 8
## Dialogue Focus Points, Textual and Dialogue Focus Points

## ACTIONS 8B

https://griffero.cl/la-dramaturgia-del-espacio/#uael-video-gallery-a40ea18-12

The following exercise awakens us to how corporeal presence, rhythm, and displacements in the space construct situations and relationships that arise without previous intention, but only because our spatial action begins to sketch legible perceptions.

4–6 participants

a) Performer 1 enters the space. Compose, define your focal point. The second participant creates a focal point on performer 1. The third participant creates a focal point on participant 1 or 2. The fourth participant creates a focal point on whichever of the previous three they choose.

Second sequence: Performer 1 reinitiates the movement and everyone follows until the group completes four sequences.

Variations: Entrances and exits, not necessarily individual, with focus dispersed according to the typology desired in whatever number of sequences. Having completed the previous exercise we realize that we constructed a narrative: the spectator will decipher the situation created according to their own perception.

b) The group repeats the exercise maintaining the same displacements and composition but this time each one adds an improvised text, corresponding to each improvised movement, that is to say, the text suggested by the sequence of images. For the first participant the text will be a soliloquy. The text should contain the development of an idea, not refer to monosyllables, nor illustrate what is realized. The situation presented will be modified by the improvised texts, but each one of these exercises can contain an infinity of texts, modifying their spatial reading.

> Let's remember that in these improvisations the text makes what is named exist, the situation or a conflict: a participant, upon saying: "Dear stepfather," "Doctor, help me," or "My love," signals the other as such, as in the same way naming a conflict or a place makes it appear, "Look how your house is burning," "Let's leave this shelter," etc.
>
> This exercise, applied to playwriting workshops, proposes that the observers elaborate texts suggested by the spatial situations and dialogues. They develop a dialogue, silence or monologue, for each movement and each performer. In this process an endless number of fictions arise from the writers' present. Then they ask the performers to repeat the sequence with the written texts.

# The Dramaturgy of the Object

Until now we've limited ourselves to defining relationships of the body with the space and haven't introduced any object on to the stage. To continue with our construction of the poetics of space, we will add to the work of the dramaturgy of the body, its union with the dramaturgy of the object.

One of the first elaborations that differentiates homo sapiens from the animals with which they cohabit this planet is the construction of objects by human beings.

Our species is recognized for its production of objects and we understand the development of civilizations in relation to the complexity of the objects that they have created. Our life is surrounded in an overwhelming manner by an endless number of objects and our existence depends upon them. We communicate, love, exterminate ourselves, develop our desires and knowledge by means of objects. In our appropriation we have given them emotional, sensual, religious, and political weight. We've impregnated them with life, signs, powers.

There is a traditional exercise that consists in asking each participant to bring an object that has special value for them and tell us its story. I point it out since by means of this exercise we see how the object brought grows in dimension, how it is imbued with emotion, memories, is valued, and gives us a sense of an object's sensitive force in a scene.

The cult of the object is something that will never end. We have constructed millions of functional and decorative objects, we've given those objects continuity and developed them over the course of history and we've impregnated in them the diverse gazes of the cultures on the planet. The object has developed defining social classes, ages, sexes, the urban, and the agrarian.

The way in which we position them and combine them creates our space, our atmosphere, our other personality. The room, as much as the scenic space, reflects a style, a personality. The quality and the distribution of the objects it contains speaks to us about who inhabits it, denotes age, social class, place, the culture and subculture we subscribe to (urban, ethnic, rural, juvenile, hippy, techno, etc.) and gives us states of being: a happy, depressed, cozy, wretched, upsetting, pacific, or aggressive room.

There are objects of nobles, beggars and millionaires, masculine and feminine adornments. There are children's, adolescent's, and executive's objects.

It's impossible to realize a typology of objects, we can only imagine the diversity and uses when we stroll through commercial centers, dispensers of objects.

Our clothing and accessories, without doubt, are among the objects that most define us, surround us, and determine us.

We reproduce nature and human constructions over and over again, in millions of objects. It is as if we wanted to appropriate the universe for ourselves by means of them. An object is given as a gift, wrapped, valued; some of them already constitute the alter ego of many.

In the object time stops and allows us to recognize the existence of the past: our toys, the lover's gift, objects of people we know, of people now gone or absent.

When we disappear the only trace left, the material footprint of our passage, will be the objects we are related to. *His armchair, her bed, their glasses, her pocketbook, his books, her diary, their collections, photographs, recorded voices, tape filmed.* Testimony of the last known material of an existence. The passage of time makes our body and epochs disappear. It is objects, architectonic constructions, that allow us to realize the material existence of the past, in the same way that dramatic and literary texts are the bitter aftertaste of previous existences.

Objects acquire a temporal "immortality," which is denied the human being. Our museums are an accumulation of objects from cultures and time periods, where the footprint left by our predecessors resides. They are the memory and patrimony of the species.

We won't analyze here the alienation the object has created in the human being, less how we make up for a desire for social climbing with a fake Louis XVI armchair. How social classes can feel superior by buying "the same" but of less quality, or how the object has become *kitsch*, in bad taste, elitist, superfluous, disposable. Or how such and such an outfit becomes fashionable. Nor will we enter into the ethical, psychic reactions that their possession creates in us, and even less into their magical characteristics, attributing them the power to transmit good or bad fortune.

The objective is only to confirm how the object is inherent to the development of art and to the perception of our surroundings and how its rearrangement even has political connotations.

Thus, the object in the space complements, informs, defines, interpolates, and becomes an irreplaceable co-actor.

# The Decontextualization of the Object

When we decide to introduce an object on the stage, we carry a world with it. Every object incorporated within a frame constitutes a reference, a sign, and is there to indicate to us a path, a place, an atmosphere, a possession, a memory, a dialogue.

The place of the object on the stage is unique and the forms of its decontextualization are part of the history of scenic language. From the way an actor has manipulated an object, or a director has decontextualized it in the scene, we can realize the parallel history of the forms of representation of universal theatre and discover the different typologies of acting based on how the body has manipulated and indicated the object in the scene.

It is important to point out that if the theatre constructs scenic artifacts to re-represent the objects of our surroundings, they enter more into the category of decorative, scenographic objects, constructed as props, or as scenery, the giant table, houses in miniature, etc.

The exercises in the dramaturgy of the object described here, will only work with the decontextualization of the concrete object, real, not with its imitation or fabrication as props. This isn't because props don't constitute an object-body dramaturgy, it's more that it corresponds to the style of a particular production.

The body in the scene doesn't exist without objects, and, even nude, there is a structure that encompasses it, a focal point that illuminates it, a space already constructed.

## The Spatial Narrtive of the Object

When an electric train runs around the scene or a solitary radio emits a song, or when there are four movie seats covered in sheaves of wheat and a gnawed picture their presence introduces us to and starts the visual narrative of the fiction. In these compositions there is only the space and the object, two narrative supports that speak for themselves only from their poetics, from their metaphysics, and remove our feelings, evoke sensations in us, our memory as much personal, as historic.

The object's presence generates a dramatic action, and we intervene with their scenic significance situating other objects around them. Those evoked by our sensibilities, those that the text suggests to us.

> A record player on a piece of furniture, its turntable turns, and vinyl records fall, on the table a canary in a cage.
> Three helium balloons and a TV transmitting the news.
> A backpack next to a toy.
> A lit standing lamp, an open book, and a telephone left off the hook.
> An aquarium, and, on the diagonal, an overturned refrigerator.

We're not interested in disemboweling meanings, we only want to attest how the decontextualized object speaks to us, proposes atmospheres, emotions, and dramatic constructions. This chapter's objective is to bring us face to face with the objects that surround us, and to consider them in terms of their artistic potential.

## Body and Object

The object relates to a body, composes with it, is part of a situation, of a text, evolves and allows the construction of scenic actions.

By means of the following exercise, we will see that according to the object that accompanies a body in the space, the reading of the

### ACTIONS 9
### Object-Body Dramaturgy

https://griffero.cl/la-dramaturgia-del-espacio/#uael-video-gallery-a40ea18-13

We ask a performer to realize an organic composition in the space. We place a revolver within reach. This picture, body and revolver, will evoke in us a series of sensations related to this image: she's going to commit suicide, he's going to kill someone.

To the same corporeal composition we add a stuffed toy in the spatial environment. The emotion evoked by the situation will change radically without the interpreter having made a single gesture to create it.

So, in succession, we will change the object and our emotional reading will be modified.

The body and a music box.
The body and a motorcycle helmet
The body and a backpack
The body surrounded by conch shells
The body and a mound of stones
The body and a guitar, etc.

situation and the emotional state it evokes in us will vary without the interpreter changing position.

Indistinctly we change the object, and our perception of the scenic narrative will transform without the interpreter's composition varying, demonstrating to us that the relationship to the object is an indispensable co-protagonist in comprehending a scenic situation.

The spatial compositions of a body with an object, and the scenic actions they construct, will be what we investigate in this chapter, adding decontextualized objects to the decontextualized body.

This process of the creative gesture in the visual construction allows us to elaborate a multitude of spatial poetics for the materialization of images the universe of the text suggests to us or for images we want to ascribe to a text to diversify its reading, or just to place the image like another verb.

We can indicate several examples by their abstraction:

A blackboard on the floor, a body writing on top of it, a woman, an electric razor hanging from her hand, a girl jumping rope.

A young woman with a baseball bat, a bicycle on the floor, a woman reading, a mechanical doll crosses the stage.

The combinations of space, body, and object are infinite, like our imagination. But these compositions create a style, an aesthetic in agreement with their spatial distribution and their evolution, since the theatre isn't a photograph, and its compositions develop over time constructing the sequential actions that arm the final narration.

The perception of the decontextualized object as object signifies an evolution in our arts of representing, performing, throughout our history. We can decipher the history of scenic styles in accord with how the stage has conceived of the relationships between body, object, and space in each period.

We won't mention in this registry of the dramaturgy of the object anything related to the art of marionettes, since they belong to a theatrical genre of their own, with ample modalities and roots in different cultures of our planet and our intention in this book isn't to analyze forms of presentation that are already structured.

Next, a simple breakdown of scenic actions and forms of decontextualizing an object in relation to a body in the theatrical space, and how the gestures are associated with diverse scenic languages.

## Body and Object in Functional Relationship

The functional object decontextualized on the stage maintains the literal utility for which it was constructed; the actor realizes scenic actions according to this functionality. An iron to iron, a glass to drink from, a lamp to decorate, cleaning one's glasses, reading a book.

A chair on the stage fulfills the same function as in our daily environment and the actor's body will make use of it according to existing cultural forms, not give it value as an "artistic artefact," nor create scenic actions with the object beyond those predefined for the functionality of that object.

Without a doubt, its decontextualization underlines for us color, design, period, style, and only refers us to a place that corresponds to the fiction, dining room chair, executive chair, a peasant's rustic chair.

In this context the object is manipulated on the basis of a literal decontextualization and the interpreter realizes compositions in accord with its daily use, utilizing it as subtext for states of being, status, or the character's psychology; the energy with which they fold or blow their nose with a handkerchief, how they will break a plate to denote aggressiveness or the way they unbutton clothes to show sensuality or boredom, is the first level of decontextualization, reflected in daily use. In brief, the relationship body-object-function is faithful to the spirit for which it was constructed. If we were to describe this body–object relationship, we would ascribe it to a naturalistic scene, where the point of the performance is to be a mirror of "reality."

I will not propose exercises with respect to this use since, besides being culturally inherent, it is part of the most habitual convention of performance. Nevertheless, we will apply it when our functional composition with the object occurs in the context of a plastic or conceptual decontextualization: someone throws stones at the theatre lights, or weaves the interior of an aquarium, or brushes themselves in a lit-up installation.

## Plastic Object-Body Dramaturgy

The object, reappropriated on the basis of its plastic decontextualization, implies relationships belonging to scenic language and born from it, and not a simple reproduction of our functional relationship. In the same way that in literary writing we associate words to create ideas and atmospheres that don't come from our use of social language—"my house is a sea of mirrors"—the approach of the body and the object as plastic scenography creates the same phenomenon.

---

### ACTIONS 10
### Plastic Object-Body Dramaturgy

https://griffero.cl/la-dramaturgia-del-espacio/#uael-video-gallery-a40ea18-14

Corporeal-organic compositions on the basis of object-plastic decontextualizations:

a) Each performer brings an object and individually realizes three plastic spatial compositions.

b) Two performers relate to each other and to the same object.

c) Three performers compose, each one with a different object.

d) Four performers create a sequence together with their objects.

e) Four performers prepare an atmospheric-object choreography, with musical ambience and/or sound.

In this exercise there is no need to indicate or focus on your own object since it constitutes part of the image and the body of the person carrying it out.

If we return to the chair as a functional element, we can see how the object takes on a dramatic atmosphere when used in its plastic form: The chair on the horizontal, a body in front of it at a distance. The chair overturned upstage, a body lying down on the diagonal. A face resting on the seat of the chair, an arm over its back.

None of these images correspond to what we see on a daily basis, since a deconstruction has interfered where body and object create a spatial poetics for us. A motorcycle, a woman undressing herself, at her side a man with a cactus.

The function of a poetics is to create associations for the spectator, where the absence of literalness leads them to participate with their senses in the perception of these compositions. The associations of the images, by themselves and as the sum of their sequences, constructs the global sense of the scene, operating like the concept of cinematic montage in its development of visual narratives (A+B=C).

In this sequence of exercises, when the interpreters displace the object spatially, they also construct a composition by doing so. The interpreter perceptibly relates to the objects avoiding any external manipulation by the stage machinery, the effect of which would annul the continuation of the narrative.

At the same time, the simple proceeding of entering with an object and situating it in the space, realized as an act that emerges from a scenic language, where the interest is in revealing our theatrical action, doesn't acquire the sensation of being staged, because it constitutes a scenic action.

We value an object's signification when the actorial manipulation of it in the scene allows us to construct sequences of plastic relationships that deliver different dramatic subtexts in accord with the actions we carry out. When a relationship between the object and the body is constructed, they occupy the same frame and are part of a global composition that allows us a perception of totality considering that the compositions, upon establishing themselves on different planes of the stage, can also realize diverse space-temporalities.

In this gesture we join two decontextualizations, that of the body and the object, that will also relate to the space according to their axes and planes.

# Body-Object and Geometry

In the same way that our body-space is a geometrical construction, objects are a geometrical construction. We should emphasize that in our construction we can underline this condition and the effect it generates within the rectangular format. Let's consider that there are objects whose form is more preponderant than their content and it is our scenic action that will revert to or underscore this condition.

The following minimal breakdown suggests examples to consider for elaborating exercises with objects and their geometric-content relationship. In each case, we can distinguish objects that are eminently functional or cultural from others that seem to appeal much more directly to the pure abstraction of geometrical form, apparently without content.

## *Objects of Circular Geometry*

In this category we differentiate between the sphere itself and that which represents a globe of the earth or a ball, for example.

## *Objects of Linear Geometry*

In geometric terms, those that create horizontal, vertical, or diagonal lines in the space: A performer traces a line across the space with adhesive tape, or their body writes with a rope that drops down to the stage from the grid, establishing diagonals, or composing with a wooden cleat or a metallic bar.

## *Objects of Rectangular Geometry*

A wooden acrylic rectangle, or a metallic sheet, can be used on the stage and their presence differentiated from boxes, chests, pictures, frames, books, mirrors, flags, and others of rectangular form.

## *Objects of Triangular Geometry*

Our abstract triangular objects are scarce, including functional ones: pennants, tables, metronomes, signage. Our composition with the triangle arises out of construction with abstract triangular elements, to which we ascribe different connotations.

## ACTIONS 11
### Geometric Object-Body Dramaturgy

https://griffero.cl/la-dramaturgia-del-espacio/#uael-video-gallery-a40ea18-15

a) With geometric objects lacking content: lines, rectangles, or circles, we construct a geometrical object choreography generating lines, vertical, diagonal, planes, etc. (compositions in sequence, work with music).

We integrate the geometry of the space, the body, and the object.

b) Actions with functional geometrical objects, both utilizing and in tension with their defined uses.

There are objects that, in relation to the body and the scenic space, prevail as geometric signs more than the significance of their function, and this is underscored according to the scenic manipulation executed by the actor with said object. In these compositions we find a similarity with the concept of abstract art, this time executed theatrically (abstract theatre).

The geometric figure also appears as an example of metaphysical ritual constructions. The first plastic representations of humanity can be seen in the Egyptian or Mesoamerican pyramids, the inscriptions on Aztec, or Mayan architecture, as well as the decorations on Pre-Hispanic, Egyptian, and African ceramics and weavings. They are as much decorative as symbolic, political, or religious. Signs of political ideologies: the swastika, shields, flags, the peace sign. The triangle as the eye of God, the cross, Buddhist shrines, and vertical minarets.

Thus, without a doubt, the gestural choreography object-stage that makes this geometry appear also references abstract sensations, or a great sensorial historical form of representation.

## The Object in its Metaphorical Function

The object on the stage can also be decontextualized, realizing a significance and use different from that it represents in daily life. Scenic language theatrically transforms the object in accordance with the scenic fiction the interpreter performs.

A box spring transformed into a boat, a toy into the body of an infant, torn paper into snow, red cloth exploding from a mouth like blood. This transposition of meaning functions as a contention and isn't the literal representation of a psychotic talking to a brick. An actor can be in dialogue with or transmit affection to an object and produce a significant change with this action.

### ACTIONS 12

Four interpreters relate to four chairs, defining the space they are in, speaking to the chairs as if they were lovers, reacting, caressing them, kissing them, making love to them, assaulting them, elaborating a transposition of a ludic meaning. The audience will participate from its perception of this ludic and conventional action.

Variation: Choose a similar object for all the participants and produce a metaphoric action.

## The Absurd Object

This is the absurd use of functional objects. This convention, for all of its place in the historical repertory of scenic objects, seems to me to be a bit tired due to its repeated use, and like a cliché of theatre of the absurd or comic sketches: the actor with the skeleton of an umbrella, the actress with a chamber pot for a hat, a toilet as a chair at the table, a toothbrush poking out of a jacket to then be used as a comb, a coat put on inside out, etc.

This tiredness certainly doesn't prevent the possibility of establishing new creative compositions for this convention, ones that will surpass the literal signs to which they have been ascribed.

# Object Nomenclature to Consider in the Exercises

## Luminous Objects

All the objects that emit light, the innumerable styles of lamps, fluorescent tubes, neon, light bulbs, headlights, bicycle lights, industrial lights, pictures and objects with interior light, decorative lights, billboards, signage panels, beacons, streetlight, parking lights, emergency lights, etc.

The luminous object allows in its composition with the actor a dramaturgy that can well constitute a scenic installation, reaching even a conceptual character. Either establishing itself as an alternative to lighting design or transforming itself into a constituent element of costuming.

The axes of the body marked by fluorescents. A space populated by standing lamps or LED figures. I separate this from lighting design since it pertains to the ambience of the scenographic construction or the global scenic installation of a montage, conditioned by a luminous infrastructure, types and quality of focus, capacity of computerized consoles, etc.

Luminous dramaturgy is a language in itself, as happens with the dramaturgy of sound. Both are fundamental elements in the construction of spatial poetics, modeling sonorous planes as much as luminous ones and influencing comprehension or the meaning of what is performed.

## The Mechanical Object

This refers to working with objects that move on their own, for their essential function, and also emit sounds that they add to the action. Juicers, vacuum cleaners, hairdryers, fans and exhaust fans, drills or electric saws, mechanical toys, remote control cars, electric trains, walking dolls, robots, etc.

## The Organic Scenic Object (Vegetable and Mineral)

Our contemporary theatre also makes plastic use of vegetable objects, fruit, plants, minerals (carbon-salt), greens, flowers, tubers.

For example, in *Brunch*, the image of a detained disappeared is comprised by a naked body with a hood over his head and a bunch of white calla lilies in his hands.

> **ACTIONS 13**
> **(Childhood) Plastic Object-Body Dramaturgy**
>
> https://griffero.cl/la-dramaturgia-del-espacio/#uael-video-gallery-a40ea18-16
>
> a) Sequence of scenic actions, textural, color, and quality atmospheres and associations with the objects in functional-plastic composition. Example: Everyone with objects of the same sign or origin: infantile, with history, industrial, from an office, hospital objects, luminous objects, sonorous, visual, domestic, masculine, feminine, decorative, religious, etc.
>
> Construct visual narratives with objects of diverse origin, quality, or texture.
>
> b) We choose a dramatic text and construct the atmosphere and scenic actions the work's universe suggests to us.
>
> c) We select a scene from a text and develop its relationship on the basis of space–object actions.

# The Dramaturgy of the Conceptual Object

The construction of a conceptual poetic space on the basis of the object on the stage is a process of deconstruction that implies realizing a gesture of double or triple decontextualization.

The development of the body–space relationship within a conceptual elaboration brings us to the generation of a third gesture, where objects represent a concept within the performance.

They don't illustrate themselves but are part of a construction that creates a third sign.

If, upon extracting an object from reality and situating it inside the rectangular format, we have generated a first decontextualization, a second gesture is to resignify it beyond its function and transform it into an object that is incorporated into scenic plasticity.

In this action, the object maintains its social unitary significance; a fan continues to be a fan. The third gesture is to transform this object into a concept: four giant fans upstage on the stage can construct a concept of space or the dramatic atmosphere of a scene, or of the character's situation-conflict.

Thus, this series of fans can refer us to death, Greek boats advancing on Troy, a character's happiness or anguish, a metaphysical place. It is an image where the object changes the atmospheric, the intangible, the global metaphor of a scene on the basis of this creative gesture. Put another way, in the first decontextualization of an object we underline its functional or historic condition. A second gesture is the body-object composition to produce atmospheres and plastic actions. In the third gesture, we produce a double or triple reading where the object no longer represents itself, isn't a sign for a literal referent, but is there to configure a third or fourth meaning that we are calling concept here and allows the amplification of the scenic alphabet towards a conceptual visual narrative.

In a certain way, it is the double reading of the literal as much as artistic composition. We know that a fact carries various readings, and they can be constructed to be perceived from various conscious-unconscious sensory layers of perception.

Here the idea is that what we perform is looking, at the same time, to represent beyond the functionality or the plastic figure of that object and, therefore, of the images and emotions of our performance.

We transform the idea that created the originating construction of that object and we give it a distinct sensory or psychic nature, transforming its reading and the perception of its meaning.

Analogically, the object in its use as concept elaborates a subtext of its own construction. This is similar to the idea of discovering the subtext of a dramatic dialogue, its other idea, that isn't part of its semantics. And, upon digging into it, we discover that the action—the dialogue or reply of the text—its dramatic motor, when seen from our appropriation finds the subtext of the subtext in a "concept" we specify. We could say that the elaboration of a conceptual image that illustrates or arises from the conception of a text has cultural antecedents in the allegorical construction, where the representations of an idea or character manifest themselves through the association of signs. An allegory that, based on various objects and corporeal and associative compositions, gives us the idea of poverty, fortune, the weather, death, or the new world.

Thus, a conceptual construction can be seen as a contemporary allegory, without already deciphered cultural symbolism, where we redefine the objects based on their literalness and their materiality.

## *The Object in a Series*

There is a gesture installed to bring us close to a mechanism for creating an object/concept onstage. This is elaborated based on the disposition of the same object in a repetitive manner onstage. This gesture interpolates us towards a conceptual reading since decontextualization in a series neutralizes the intrinsic reading particular to it, so that the sum of the signs carries us to a perceptive association, producing a second reading of this scenic composition.

A helium balloon or a picture don't establish the same perception as eight balloons with four intertextual pictures onstage: this confronts us with a poetics and an atmosphere that proposes sensations to us and evokes them within us.

A gesture and its intention to interpolate us speaks to us from a different place: a series of speakers, a row of medical cabinets, four identical pieces of furniture, five refrigerators, four electric trains, etc. The object in series moves away from the concrete representation of the object and references a concept for us.

Which concept? That which emerges, in the case of theatre based on the textual, from the interpretation of the work, or that which arises from the association of images in the case of a visual and sensory representation.

The process of conceptual creation is infinite, and the example of the series is just one element of construction. The decontextualization of an object in relation to the decontextualization of another is also a process of conceptual association and, seen globally, takes us to a more complex development of the scenic installation.

## *Objects in Association from a Conceptual Gesture*

Where we want to transform the idea or situation in a conceptual scenic composition, we elaborate a poetics of space based on this notion with the creative gesture already established. This gesture is an action, it amplifies the forms of writing in the space appealing to associations and perceptions that allow the reformulation of representations of reality based on an imaginary that is nourished by other forms of writing to develop a narrative.

The transformation of our space into a conceptual space, born from our vision of the dramatic work, implies a diversification of corporeal compositions with the object and the development of actors' scenic actions that emerge from this relationship and the definition of this visuality like that of a conceptual theatre.

All of our scenic patrimony could be restated in its dramatic universe based upon a conceptual reading of the same. In the same way that there is a contemporary reading that is based on the text's structure and proposes a conceptual representation.

For the basic and illustrative form of the body-object-concept composition, the following examples:

> An armchair in the middle of a child's pool, surrounded by luminous plastic roses, a man knits on the sofa.
>
> Three ironing boards, on top of them a red costume, below them a woman with red shoes, playing a flute.
>
> A row of wheat, in between them two teardrop lamps.
>
> A dried tree hangs upside down, below leaves and apples.
>
> A mound of carbon, on top of it a television playing the image of fire.

These can be conceptualized as well in other compositions with the clothes the interpreter wears, their actions, and the resulting associations: three microphones with pedestals, a young woman dressed for a party wearing boxing gloves sings, a military man in a country scene. A palm tree, a character wearing Andean dress and holding a luminous placard, upstage an iron bookcase on top of him, a naked woman with a carnival mask and a flower.

## The Actors' Conceptual Scenic Actions

With this term we refer to the dramatic character's actions realized by one or several actors in their work with objects, generating their own spatial poetics. I say their own, to differentiate them from scenic actions that are part of the scenographic effects of montage (a line of light crosses the space or demolishes a stained-glass window). An action that materializes in the interior of the character, the other verb of the text translated into an image, amplifying the readings of their condition or the conflict in a situation.

It's an action that transpires onstage, where the spectator sees its construction, and the transformation of meaning that emerges.

We keep constantly referring to an action onstage, with our body and with objects: functional, plastic, etc. Each proposed exercise brings us once again to actions, like all the historic development of scenic art.

When the interpreter knits and throws his needles, when he destroys a diary, or serves a cup of tea, bodily compositions are generated with the others. Without a doubt we are confronted by multiple and innumerable scenic actions.

Conceptual scenic actions of contemporary theatrical montages find their references in the *happenings* or art actions that form a constituent part of the history of *performance* and in the interventions of conceptual visual artists, where they use their own body or that of others as a constituent part of the work.

Integrating these manifestations into a theatrical montage is what I designate as conceptual scenic actions. We could also call them performative actions, since they produce the sensation of a unique fact, and of a situation that happens in the present where the spectator participates in the construction of that gesture and where they participate in the construction of the convention.

Asking ourselves what action the interpreter will execute in such a scene or situation; we would amplify our poetics, reverting to a construction of images that arise from a conceptual creation.

A show can center itself or partially intervene through these scenic actions, that in a certain way will refer us to the same conceptual and sensory universe of the performance, but that don't follow its principles, integrating it as an expression of the interior of the theatrical artistic format, thus changing the definition of this gesture, transforming itself into a constituent part of the development of the scenic language. This narrative, as much visual as from dramatic writing, becomes "Conceptual Theatre."

The scenic actions in a performance that isn't essentially visual, emanate from the text, the paratext or the silences of dramatic writing and aren't necessarily related to the author's stage directions, but emerge from the construction of a montage and from the intertexts that constitute it.

The foregoing doesn't imply a formal or arbitrary construction. On the contrary, its objective is to establish new emotional relationships, to give a larger representative spectrum to the dramatic tensions, thereby producing a more active participation of the spectator's unconscious when psychically connecting or deciphering the multiple levels upon facing the proposed image. This work is an inherent part of the development of our scenic language, in its search to give diverse perspectives to the thematics of our existence.

Vicente Huidobro's creative conception has always resonated for me. He pointed out that it wasn't the subject or the new theme that generated a contemporary creative act in itself, that is to say that it wasn't enough to name airplanes in poetry for it to become "new," if the author described the airplane the same way that Victor Hugo described it, for example. If the structure is maintained as "old," we would equally perceive the new from a pre-established perception. Thus, in a dramatic text or a scenic composition, naming or introducing contemporary objects doesn't mean that the work will produce for us a contemporary visuality if our writing or scenic action references structures corresponding to styles or modes of creativity already defined. Therefore, even though a television series introduces contemporary themes, conflicts, is daring, it's still a television series, given the primacy of its narrative formation.

Let's consider that putting these notions into practice—body-object concept and the scenic actions that derive from it—will always maintain as its ultimate end the generation of an internal line elaborated to realize the convention of a scenic truth.

In all dramatic action, the great challenge is the construction of scenic truth, so that our narration isn't impregnated with a sterile fantasy or showy character, or that the effect produced becomes false, established, predictable. We don't necessarily feel aggression because an interpreter appears with electric drills in each of his hands and his torso red with blood. Perhaps the effect generated for us is more one of refusal, or preoccupation for the manipulation the actor makes of them, more than the truth of the emotion or conflict he intended to produce.

To realize exercises of scenic actions, let's avoid considering big constructions. The basic idea of this book is to deliver tools for the development of creation but from a place that is accessible in terms of material possibilities, based on elements at our disposal in our immediate surroundings.

We'll place our bet on maintaining the artisanal condition of our art and the possibility or capacity of its execution for all those who feel a passion for it, without the necessity of preconditions such as grand stages or budgets in order to generate our proposals for renewal.

## ACTIONS 14
### Conceptual Actions (Maritime Atmosphere)

https://griffero.cl/la-dramaturgia-del-espacio/#uael-video-gallery-a40ea18-17

## ACTIONS 14B
### Conceptual Actions (Object-Body Series)

https://griffero.cl/la-dramaturgia-del-espacio/#uael-video-gallery-a40ea18-18

## ACTIONS 14C
### Conceptual Actions (Urban-Light)

https://griffero.cl/la-dramaturgia-del-espacio/#uael-video-gallery-a40ea18-19

## ACTIONS 14D
## Conceptual Actions (Latin American Citation)

https://griffero.cl/la-dramaturgia-del-espacio/#uael-video-gallery-a40ea18-20

Construction of body-object-concept relationships

a) Based upon a visual association:

Starting with objects in a series elaborate a sequence with a sonorous universe.

Starting with an association of objects, construct conceptual actions and atmosphere.

b) Based on an idea or a text:
Starting with a proposed theme, let's elaborate its conceptual atmosphere and the scenic actions that derive from it.

Construct sequences in which the scenic actions are of a conceptual character.

c) Working from a dramatic text or scene, elaborate its conceptual universe.
In the sequences you may integrate simultaneous conceptual scenic actions.

In conceptual composition we sometimes get confused with respect to whether or not creative gestures of the conceptual body–object relationship shouldn't be classified as symbolist representations and why don't we define them as such? From a semantic or psychoanalytic perspective, we are producing symbols that come from our sensory associations. Then, if it is a fundamental antecedent, in terms of what defines a symbolist composition in accord with the historic movement and its creators, its intention comes from a structural conception very different from that of theatrical language.

In the scenic creations of the twentieth century the creative proposals of Maeterlinck and the stagings of Meyerhold are certainly renovators of the preceding poetics of space, in the same way as the utilization of objects by the Futurist Movement, which introduced industrial materials and objects onstage, neon or rubber. Also, the Surrealist movements, that through their object gesture refer to the presence of the unconscious.

In turn, the poetics of space based upon concepts nourishes the intrinsic analogy between the conceptual art of the visual arts and that of scenic language, besides being complemented by innumerable visual arts that participate in the creation of productions.

The relationship is such that, when attending an exhibition of contemporary visual arts, we have no difficulty judging it using various readings that we associate with the visual conceptualization of a dramatic text. This is also facilitated by the three-dimensional construction of some installations, that allow us to relate them to compositions for a scenic space.

# Objects of Scenic Artifice as Concepts

The history of the stage gives us an infinity of elements of representation that, in their first use, only refer to the original or historic artifact and its functionality, but the reutilization of these from a conceptual (postmodern) place introduces them once more to the scenic space, as a citation of theatricality and their own illusory artifact. In the nineteenth century theatrical frame, the painted curtain, wings that forced perspective, flats of ocean waves, clouds, moons created changes of scene, allowing the figuration of the places of representation.

All these elements of stage machinery, as well as their equipment, ropes, beams, appear as plastic-conceptual elements of theatricality in their new decontextualization. A beam, with or without lights, in the interior of the performance space, or the complete grid that descends to the level of the interpreters and transforms the scene, reintroduce themselves as scenic objects liberated from their primary functionality without necessarily annulling it, in order to constitute themselves as part of the fiction.

The red curtain stripped of its functionality is also re-introduced as a scenic citation or a plastic-conceptual object. The unveiling of scenographic structures, their panels and all the artifacts proper to the historic illusionism of the stage, decontextualizes and transforms them into object signs of a poetics: The countryside curtain, torn and slanted as a backdrop, behind it birdcages, in front of the curtain a girl seated on a carriage, with her typewriter beneath her arm.

## Animals in the Dramaturgy of Space

The condition of an animal as a live body onstage decontextualized from its environment represents itself to us unfolding an infinite number of signs. We haven't reached the point, like in film, of transforming it into an actor or protagonist. But its eruption does acquire a scenic presence, it is a live organism in movement, to which we attribute emotional weight and with which we establish a particular dialogue, that inscribes it as a dramatic character.

The presence of animals onstage, when not part of a circus, fulfills a dramatic role in relation to the gaze of the spatial poetics into which it is inserted. In a functional or naturalistic theatre, the animal is a decoration of the habitat the mimesis creates. A lion in a circus, chickens in a chicken coop, horses in a stable or pulling a carriage, or as someone's mascot.

In a plastic composition peacocks against a blue background, a tiger in a suspended cage, trained falcons flying about the stage, etc. are part of the dramatic content with which we construct scenic actions. They also acquire a conceptual role, where the animal not only represents itself, but is the concept of a fable.

Starting with my first text I have introduced the presence of animals into each work that I've written, in order to establish conflicts, metaphors, and emotional relationships as much dramatic as conceptual. Not for aesthetic considerations, but from a social perception that the presence of animals in Western urban settings shows how relations between human beings and their mascots acquire deep emotional dimensions, where dialogues, furies, pains, loves, color intimate manifestations, are at times of greater value than those of their social relationships. Let's not forget their condition of being our cohabitants on this planet: they are also earth dwellers.

Violeta Espinoza, a theatrical researcher who has investigated the presence of animals and their dramatic interactions in writing about my works, refers to the symbolic concept associated with the salmon in *Midday Lunches or Petit Dejeuner du Midi*, pointing out: "They swim against the current, like the condemned: they leave no trace behind, like the disappeared; they are each isolated in their fishbowl, like the tortured; they live in long, thin fishbowls, like Chileans in a long, narrow strip of land... "

In the show *Your Desires in Fragments*, tarantulas run across the bodies of the speakers and in the face of death, the final text concludes with the sentence: "Don't worry, I'll feed the spiders." The conceptualizations of this image vary and have cultural and symbolic antecedents; the spider at the center of the web, as a symbol of the world, from where it takes care of the world, saves creation, and maintains the possible continuation of human beings, signifying cycles of transformation.

# Conceptual Acting

In acting terms, the forms of composition of the body and the construction of the actor's theatrical signs or actions will be modified according to the construction of the poetics of space elaborated from the text and the multiple situations where relationships with scenic objects emerge.

Using the paradigms of modernity these aesthetics can be recognized or analyzed on the basis of how they represent scenic actions in their relationship with objects, as well as defining the styles employed on the basis of the actor's gesture and the spatial composition of the scene.

As part of their impetus for constructing viewpoints and languages historical vanguards redefined or resignified the dramaturgy of the body-object. In postmodern theatre all the cultural baggage of the stage is liberated from referring to its original model, the same happens with the dramaturgy of the object and its relationship with the sign and the body onstage.

In contemporary staging, the body-object composition can vary indistinctly. Thus, the actor can act and react and relate in a functional manner, plastic and conceptual within the same performance.

We have to underscore that everything described takes place in a continual search for the construction of a theatre as mirror or microscope of our surroundings that no longer arises out of a literal reproduction of reality but is constructed on the basis of how the author, through scenic language, shapes their vision of reality elaborating it as a politics of art.

Conceived in this way we see no opposition between realistic and conceptual acting, dilemma of the twentieth century and traditional scheme of some centers of theatre training, where the branch of realistic acting is articulated in opposition to non-realistic. The body, its gestures, its voice and its emotions will always be realistic and should emerge from scenic truth. Fear is fear, love is love beyond the poetics of space that encompasses it. Acting Medea is not more realistic when wearing Greek dress, relating to objects functionally, than a Medea on top of an automobile between brambles and accompanied by children asphyxiating themselves. The text and emotions will be maintained as identical in their nature. What will change will be the gestures and the scenic compositions that elaborate them.

Each Dramaturgy of Space will generate its typologies of acting, as creations of its corporeal-object scenic actions. And all aspire to get an interpretation of the "real."

In this way, between the nomenclatures used to define the acting that a body onstage develops, they can approach the construction of a character, an icon, a role, a speaker, a typology that will name the forms of interpretation of the scenic other.

This typology will arise out of what we establish in the creation of our scenic convention, so that each spectacle will develop its own or referential actorial conception.

For the needs of the dramatic structure of the play *Your Desires in Fragments* and to single out the forms of construction of the other, the interpreters defined themselves on the basis of their stage directions as speakers: "*Where each body assumes diverse voices, there are voices that return to emerge from forgotten bodies, there are others that are memories of others speaking through your body, there are voices that are registers-recordings. There are speakers in the present—from the past and other of desire.*"

The acting typology that this text suggested had as its purpose a form of acting where the interpreter could break away from a continuous, unique personification and situate themselves in a place where a thought could evolve, succeeding in modifying space temporally in accord with the text altering its dialogue and place depending upon where it was spoken. The foregoing doesn't necessarily establish itself as a model for conceptual acting. I make this clarification to avoid the search for an emotion, a voice, or a manual on conceptual acting. We are defining preliminary categories for some elements of the scenic alphabet that allow us to think about the languages of our representations and of dramatic writing.

# Actorial Body and Appropriation of a Place of Fiction

In the abstraction of the empty space it is the actor's body that refers us to the place the fiction represents. In our environment, our body modifies itself, acts and reacts in accord with a sum of factors: age, condition, social hierarchy, emotion, or state of being, our present, the situation in which we are living, the characteristics of the ambience where we find ourselves.

These distinctions, in general terms, condition the specificity of the place and the role we represent/perform inside those spaces (room, hospital, cell, train, car, police station, street, tunnel, patio, skyscraper, terrace), as well as our insertion in a period of a nation, historical context, or the atmosphere of the space, added to the geography of the place (desert, woods, beach, mountain), that are besides inserted in a temporality, schedule and season (day, twilight, winter, summer).

When a body enters a scene in the situations of an action that is born from a place, it should imbue itself with all the characteristics that performance of the fictional place implies, making the existence of that place possible. This allows the performer to amplify his actions and reactions and to nourish the modifications of his corporeal kinesthesia at the same time. Otherwise, we would barely perceive a body onstage trying to express emotions.

Living a scenic fiction, you will see the stars, feel the night cold, the breeze will whip your face, your vision will run across the immensity, you will see silhouettes and the visualization of your psyche will impregnate itself in the emotions of your body. The spectator will not decipher your visualizations but will participate in the convention and will perceive a body that interpolates us from another dimension.

Our body moves and reacts, talks, feels, in relation to a certain spatial temporality where it finds itself. And the text, situating the word and the emotion in the context of the dimension of this place and situation, will have an organic repercussion in the body.

Gestures, emotions, the nuances of words, bodily subtexts will have an internal origin upon situating them in concordance with the place where the action happens. To say: "I love you" on a beach in summer, at night in the middle of a cold forest, between the sheets in a room, whispered in a public place, as a goodbye at the airport, or in front of someone dying on the highway will give us the specific emotional register of that phrase. One that doesn't arise from the boards of a stage but from the place in which I insert myself within the fiction performed.

Recognizing the place from where it speaks allows the body, its voice and atmosphere, to become organic, and therefore, carry a larger grade of veracity than enunciating a text without personal experiences of the place from where it is emitted. This place doesn't necessarily have to be illustrated in the space, but yes in the imaginary of the person who acts.

We are speaking here about theatricality and not film, where the actor is generally contained by the location and its characteristics and integrates himself organically into those surroundings: walking on the beach, the sand influences the body, seeing the sea, feeling the wind, the sun's rays reflected on your face, your body shivering upon feeling the freezing water.

The theatre actor on the other hand, has to make all of that exist in the rectangular space. Given that the scenic format of the fictional place doesn't exist in the empty space, the actor brings us to that place, visualizes it, gives it its characteristics, projects it.

The process of internal visualization is the basic technique by which to receive the stimuli of the place and transmit its sensations through our corporeal-emotional reactions.

We can predetermine with what emotion I enter a place, but then the temporal continuity of the fable will make it so that the situation will develop, and the modification of the fictional place will give hues and breaks to that emotion, in agreement with how our visualization evolves.

The visualization allows us to develop scenic corporeal actions that arise from this action to give form and content to an emotion. The text will give us the facts about the situation and the emotion that should emerge, but not how we should construct them.

Faced with a scene where you have to manifest desperation, the visuality we make emerge, compromising feelings and sensations, will guide us and will develop the actions and reactions of our body and our voice. If an actress visualizes dozens of spiders approaching her in a place, she will have a reaction that modifies it, even more if she feels that they are invading her body. The emotional corporeal action will modify her kinesics. As she feels them entering her mouth and altering her speech images will be proposed and will transform the emission of her text.

It isn't a question of the spectator deciphering the visualization in question, but they should feel this body convulsing, establishing a scenic truth with its acting. The production that envelopes the actor strengthens and contributes to her visualization process. Although scenery mimetically describes the place, or refers to it, there won't be night falls, history, cold, nor anything beyond the physical "from a horizon with its mountains," nor the psychic planes of the interpreter's internal life in it.

At the same time, the fictional place doesn't necessarily imply the construction of concrete places—there are mental spaces, metaphysical, abstract. The scenic space as a fictional format can also represent an emotional place, the residue of an atmosphere, the space of a non-existent dimension, a fragment of an idea. By mentioning the concept of a fictional place, we are referring to this amplitude of spaces, and to maintain them the actor must recreate its imaginary geometry and the multiple spaces that can cohabit onstage in order to be able to define the place where they act.

To transmit the fictional place in which the actor's body is immersed, they construct it by means of a sensibility that interweaves the scenic space, its laws, and the fictional place they are transmitting.

Thus, they will realize real motivations from surroundings that will allow them to create organically the diversity of their emotional states, that will modify the sentences they speak and will give us our way of walking, compositions, looks, emotions, and the atmosphere from which to situate the text.

It is fundamental to distance us from an interpretation that, by defect, conceives of the stage as the place from where you act, since instead of being guided by the temporal spatial coordinates of the fiction, our body will adapt itself in relation to the spatial coordinates and composition of the stage.

Given that the organicity of our immediate present determines our movements, displacements, gestures, and emotional energies that are developed in that present (of the stage), we shouldn't forget that the play contains another space time, that establishes a reordering by the actor of the spatial temporality in accord with the fiction.

Nevertheless, there are options for scenic creation that establish the stage as the place of performance as an option, with its limits and in its present, and are guided by the abstract narrative laws of the rectangular format that decontextualizes itself to transform itself into a fictional space. The scenic space can contain a place of fiction as much as an infinite number of simultaneous places and, based on their different planes, can represent places in disparate times, whether in the sequence of performance or in the same present.

A place, a present: a hospital. Three places, a present: first plane a park, second plane a room, third plane a beach (simultaneous framed presents or in succession).

Three diverse space-temporalities in one present: first plane 1940 a child plays, second plane 1970 a couple dances, third plane nineteenth century a romantic character commits suicide.

We will cover the complexity of this chapter on the basis of a simple construction. In this first approximation let's consider the totality of the rectangle as container of a single place.

## ACTIONS 15

Exercises of visualization and temporal planes.
Define places to perform and work the atmospheric visualization.
Work with ambient sound.
Template of examples
A place in the country: Two people on a train line. I determine its route in the space, it's a diagonal.

> I visualize its placement: The line crosses a mound between fields of wheat, the end of the diagonal a tunnel. Upstage the horizon of hills and sun.
> I visualize its spatial temporality and texture: Summer, afternoon, the tracks shine, refuse between the ties.
> I construct the actions: The sun wrinkles my eyes, I play with my shadow, I lie down on the tracks, I open my hands, the other person balances on the tracks, I sit at their side, caress them, a plane fumigating passes, birds fly, etc.

To situate a fictional place in the empty scenic space, we have to visualize it in relation to the coordinates of the rectangle, and its projection beyond that. If I enter a church, I first situate its formal distribution—where is the altar, the corridors, the lateral altars. I determine where the light enters, the height of the columns, then I define the temporality of the place: season of the year, hour, temperature, day, etc. I consider my emotional objective and reason for being there (I come desolated to plead, timidly to rob, lovingly to meet with someone).

The place visualized, the body begins to nourish itself from its atmosphere, textures: the floor creaks because its wood, or is frozen if its marble. I smell odors, my focal points reveal the surroundings. Someone prays, a cockroach passes. I look towards the church's arches, the body organically turns in relation to the place and modifies its state of being, asphyxiates. Its state of being is fed by sensitive information.

The fictional place doesn't illustrate (in pantomime terms), it is felt and reflected in our actions and reactions. The spectator should participate in this world, since they can't guess internal sensations.

Everything should manifest itself as a subtle echo of the internal, without revealing a game of illustrative riddles. At the same time, the interpreter activates their body in accord with the characteristics of the imagined place. In a continuous spatial sequence, the change in fictional places performed doesn't imply leaving the scenic space and beginning another sequence.

> **ACTIONS 16**
>
> Parallel fictional spaces in a same temporality.
> We'll utilize the diverse planes of the space and assign them places:
> A performer jumps rope (on a patio).
> Two performers are in an amorous sequence in a forest
> A third performer on another plane, sees
> what is happening in the scene from an abstract place.
> A fourth draws.
>
> Having created these displacements, they re-situate themselves in other planes in the space taking their fictional places with them.
> Variation: We generate parallel fictional places. After establishing the first convention, the performers define a second place of collective encounter common to all. Disintegrating the autonomous spaces transforming it into a collective one: they meet again on the deck of a boat looking at the stars.

In this way the different isolated places of the performers are transformed into a common atmospheric place, which they then take apart to return to their preceding place, which will imply changes of states of being, corporealities, and emotions as they realize the transfers of spatial planes.

In this exercise all of the performers are perceived in a present, in parallel places. If we want to underline the difference in the planes in terms of diverse historical periods, the dramaturgy of the object as much as that of the costuming will lead us to this convention.

If we have a young man injecting heroin on one plane and Prometheus chained on another, we dig deeper into the cohabitation of fictional planes in the space, and we can perform it as a unity or as autonomous fragments.

## The Fictional Place as Concept

We shape the scenic space, as the support of the infinite fictions that construct theatricality, according to the infinity of gestures of creation that elaborate the poetics of text and space.

In general terms, the scenic tradition for representing texts has covered diverse constructions and materialities that have appeared in relation to our material evolution.

It has decontextualized or re-contextualized forms and visualities that arise from our surroundings and in the parallel development generated by the contributions of architecture or the visual or virtual arts.

The scenographic evolution occurred in parallel with the development of dramatic texts and advances in concepts of staging. Psychological realism and the necessity for functional actions populated scenic spaces with living rooms, waiting rooms, diverse chairs, armchairs, beds, where the body could lie down, sit, or stretch out. Kitchens, bars for pouring drinks, bookcases from which to take books, or chests, pianos, trunks.

Scenic architecture, initiated by Symbolism, gave the stage heights, columns, staircases, cubes, geometric elements that recomposed bodies and proposed by means of these forms, volumes, and lines, elements that generated an atmosphere that referenced the feelings of the work.

Russian Constructivism created scenographies in works where the scenic structure didn't end by defining habitual references, but introduced the structural scaffolding of a construction that in itself was a form, relating more to the scene and the possibility of structuring planes and corporeal compositions, and scenic movements on diverse planes, than to the traditional functional compositions of the preceding period.

Other theatre has opted to use real spaces as fictional places: facades of buildings, bodegas, train stations, parking lots, a beach, giving a pre-existing location to the performance fable and gifting it with a new form of material veracity as support.

The scenic space as concept for theatrical language also appears as a place for the poetics of space, with the space understood as supporting scenic actions that constitute the fiction and not as supporting the representation of places. Where the scene functions in relation to the rules of its own geometry, to the choreography of bodies in relation to the space and themselves, or with the introduction of objects that already fulfill a function in the structuring of this global choreography, where the isolated kitchen is part of the performative action.

But we can't disentangle our contemporary perception of the rectangular scenic narrative given the appearance of the visual cinematographic narrative. This format allows us to amplify scenic language, from its writing as much as from its visual narrative.

# Cinematification of the Stage Theatricalization of Film

The concept of cinematification of the stage arises from a creative gesture that takes the visual narrative of film and disarms it, to reconstruct it as part of the alphabet of theatrical language. In this definition we aren't referring to projecting images or audiovisual material on the stage, nor to film excerpts, digital medias, or transmediality that dialogues onstage.

We are referring to how in the evolution of our scenic art, as much in the writing of a text as in its palatial narrative, the stage is fed by and appropriates cinematographic narrative, restructuring it to fit the codes of theatrical language.

This, incorporated into the scenic creative gesture, is converted into a language of another convention, amply perceptible, since the spectator's reading has evolved in parallel with the conventions of cinematographic narratives.

This process is intrinsic to both forms of narration given that they constitute themselves on the basis of the rectangular format. All development implies broadening the capacities of visual narratives that are constructed using that format and echo in both manifestations, in the back and forth between film and theatre, where the spatial-temporal specificities and the three dimensionality of scenic art are maintained. Deducing that, in this transposition, it acquires in its theatricality connotations and forms of performance that belong to its art.

The development of cinematography in the twentieth century increased the visual narrative possibilities of the rectangle to relate emotions, thoughts, discourses, and stories to us.

The concepts of montage, editing structures, fragmenting vision in planes, frames, angles, camera movements, rhythmic and continuity concepts, freezing the image, reversing and forwarding, along with the concept of visual writing or filmscript, its structure of narrative levels for a spatial temporal story, simultaneous past and present (*racconto*), ellipsis, the relationship between image, sound, and fable—these are all techniques used imaginatively to renovate our vision of reality.

The Dramaturgy of Space assimilates this development to integrate it on to the stage, proposing that all the contributions of cinematographic narrative have possible recodifications in theatrical language.

Thus, this conception gives us other approaches to the narrative possibilities of the stage space. It conceives of them from different angles and in constant transference and subdivision. It liberates us from an approximation that only takes into account the concrete physical-geometrical limits of rectangularity, creating a perspective that visualizes the stage using an invisible imaginary narrative.

Confronted with the stage rectangle we can imagine it to be the big viewfinder of a fixed camera that waits to be manipulated, turned on its tripod, moved on a dolly. It fragments angles and planes and contains infinite narrative spatial temporalities that amplify the scenic alphabet in all its signs: acting, lighting, writing.

The scenic rectangle can also contain in its frame a spatial temporality greater than the plane of the camera. In a single frame the scenic space can make us see simultaneous fictional spaces and a variety of places in diverse temporalities.

Such a construction allows me to develop dramatic writing whose structure can expand into diverse temporal dimensions. A structure that, in its turn, resolves the performance challenges created by presenting multiple scenes in a single form. In *Downstream* we see the actions in each apartment of a three-story building, plus the situations that happen on the riverbank and the subdivisions of multiple spatial temporal narratives all at once.

In *Cinema Utoppia* the actors' actions that develop within the cinematographic screen—that is itself a theatre stage—their spatial composition, temporal changes, ellipses, and soundtrack, make us perceive it as if it were a film, when in reality it is theatrical language that reproduces a visual language that refers to a cinematographic style. These resources allow a cinematification of the stage.

Perceiving the stage rectangle as the viewfinder of a camera allows theatricality to contain and narrate all the imaginable dimensions and to auto-relate itself according to changes in the text, without the necessity of illustrating those distinct times or places. It also helps to introduce a multi-narrative spatial-temporal visualization of the story and in the structural dynamics of the dramatic text.

Past, present, and future coexist in the stage space, as the parallel dimensions of our psyches, planet, and universe. Thus, the cinematification of the stage amplifies and opens horizons for the creative elaboration of The Dramaturgy of Space. It gives a range of tools to dramatic writing as much as to the spatial poetics of its performance and deepens the symbiosis between narrative writing and the artistic elaborations of the visual narrative.

## The Planes of the Body and Spatial Temporal Dimensions

The rectangle contains all times within its spatial narrative. Thus, entrances and exits, or opening and closing the curtain, aren't necessary to show changes in spatial temporalities. Lighting, sound, and text certainly contribute to our comprehension of these displacements.

Our linear conception and personal experiences of time are reproduced in the spatial temporal geometry of the stage. From that we can establish the convention: the area upstage is regularly established as the place of the past, while the frontal plane is that of the future (or vice versa, eventually).

In general, the present is usually determined by the place where an action begins. This reading is determined in relation to the axes of the body and its spatial placement.

A place onstage implies a unity of time. The body is in a place, in this present (without considering the universe of mental times). The conventional reading of the spatial narrative is that the present is always contained in the body. As a constant presence it moves its present to different spatial temporalities when it moves.

### *Basic Past–Present Relationship by Spatial Geometry*

Some dramatic structures contain anachronisms in their telling, analepsis (*flashback*), simultaneous past and present (*racconto*), or advances to the future (*flash-forward*) as parallel cohabitations of dimensions, physical or mental places. Based on the geometric narrative of the rectangle, we can establish conventions that allow the representation of these narrative forms.

When a body is installed at a point onstage, what is situated at its back can construct the convention of a situation of different spatial temporality than the performer: the image of a memory.

An actor focuses internally, thinking about her childhood, and a child with balloons appears at the back of the stage. The difference in planes (behind, before) allows us to see this composition as the character's past. If the child with balloons is on the same stage plane as the actor, it will be part of her present, and even if for dramaturgical fiction you tried to construct another temporality, it would be difficult to sustain it scenically in this position.

In our perception of these two temporal planes the kinesics of the body in the present that materializes a past becomes fundamental. The relationship of one to the other deepens this perception for us. Thus, I can visualize from my present a past situation and enter into a dialogue with it, signaling the change by simultaneously presenting the past and present in a single scene (representing thinking about the past), where the past is brought into the present. All of this causes changes in the spatial relationship.

An example of the simultaneous presentation of past and present (*racconto*) in the play *Ecstasy* is when the character Andrés remembers his dead mother on his birthday in his room, and the mother appears upstage with a cake, and from his room he speaks to his mother. I speak to the past from my present.

In the flashback or forward, as we suggested above, the performer integrates or evokes the space of the other temporal situation and then returns to the space of his present. In *Downstream*, a character threatens another with what will happen to him if he betrays him: simultaneously, we see the execution of a young man. Then, the dialogue is picked up again. In this way a flash-forward is inserted into the scene.

The corporeal convention that exists for these cases facilitates the reading of these changes in temporal planes. It facilitates our visual reading of the text in performance.

## *Changing the Body's Axis to Displace Different Fictional Planes*

If I define the scenic planimetry according to planes of time and different places, I can go beyond the diverse dimensions of the geometry of space. Displacement of the body produces an ellipsis that transports it to the spatial temporalities of the convention applied. The body turns on its axis, towards the left side, and then does so in the opposite direction in order to realize this convention.

The body thus produces an effect, like a dissolve, by means of its corporeality, that isn't limited to its formal turning, and should be joined to a change in its kinetic content as another environment is visualized and the body resituates itself in that environment. In the first frontal plane we are in a jail, we realize a half turn to the left, we take the horizontal and we're walking along a street, or through the forest, or the desert, etc. As we turn the dissolve produces a change in the plane of the body's axis and direction, establishing in this way change of place and time.

In the staging of *Ecstasy*, three actors walked through a park on the horizontal, at the center they turned and continued along the vertical, creating the convention of going along a street. Upon arriving at the back of the stage they turned again, and arranged themselves in a circle, situating themselves in the apartment of one of them.

In a certain way, we produce the ellipses of film with our bodies. The kinesics turn and change is a necessary complement to this technique, since advancing in a straight line continues to maintain our present.

## ACTIONS 17
## Examples of Cinematification in Productions: *Ecstasy or Steps to Sainthood, Downstream, Midday Lunches or Petit Dejeuner du Midi, End of the Eclipse,* and *Cinema Utoppia*

https://griffero.cl/la-dramaturgia-del-espacio/#uael-video-gallery-a40ea18-21

### Simultaneous past and present (*racconto*) exercise
To define the temporal planes we establish different situations for an interpreter in the present and his spatial dialogue with a situation or figure from the past. Interpreter 1 is in a situation in the present, Interpreter 2 is on a plane and situation from the past.

> **Linear ellipsis exercise**
> By means of turning the body on its axis we establish changes of planes and places as a continuation of the linear narrative.
>
> **Analepsis (flashback) exercise**
> Change the axis to move yourself to a time and place from the past.

Another instance for producing the convention of the flashback, without changing the actor's axis, consists of making it emerge from the actor's corporeal figure: the interpreter creates a composition that references someone they evoke, allowing their memory to introduce the characters and situation evoked by their memory into the space: remembering a discussion, the interpreter integrates themselves into the evocation of the past, and then that dissolves, not only because the sequence ends, but through the interpreter's gesture, which retakes the same composition and plane as that from which the memory was evoked, returning to the first temporality.

In *Cinema Utoppia*, the interpreter, from his emotional and corporeal composition, remembers an amorous situation on the beach, the evocation materializes, the character appears, they live the scene, the situation ends, and the actor retakes the original composition, resituating himself in the former present and continuing the narrative in its linearity. These changes can certainly be complemented with lighting, scenographic, and audiovisual effects, and by the narrative of the text as opportunities present themselves.

Another scenic application derived from cinematification is that of the frozen image, when an action is suspended with the object of maintaining dramatic tension, to stop time or reveal the instantaneous thought of an actor.

We can add the process of generating a scenic situation that produces the backing up effect (turning back or rewind): In the production of *99 La Morgue*, the actors retreat from a scene's present, acting marching back, resituating the action in a preceding sequence and from there taking up the driving thread of the narrative again.

At the same time, a relevant contribution has been the concept of the soundtrack of cinematography where diverse sonorous planes coexist. Atmospheric sounds and meanings are mixed with musicalization. In its theatricalization, this allows a dramatic sequence narrated in imagistic actions that can be developed in a larger sequence of time, such that rhythmic, visual, and sonorous choreography, along with the actor's movements, replaces the verb. In the writing and staging of *Cinema Utoppia*, the totality of the last scene centered on this resource, while in *Downstream* this procedure is intermixed with brief texts.

The possibility of recording scenes, uploading them to a computer, and constructing a soundtrack[1] that follows the action refers us to a sonorous cinematographic conception. At the same time, the development of amplification technology and the use of small microphones, installed in different places onstage, can amplify the sound of actions, the manipulation of objects, steps, voices, breathes, etc. giving new meanings and possibilities to the idea of reality onstage.

## ACTIONS 18
## Theatricalization of Film Scenes

https://griffero.cl/la-dramaturgia-del-espacio/#uael-video-gallery-a40ea18-21

This exercise serves us as the application of the concept of theatricalization of cinematographic narrative and proposes acting, spatial, and compositional challenges by translating film

---

[1] "The Grifferian vision is of a reality-prison, of an art boxed-in that locks the spectator in rectangles. Only one art exists that escapes the rectangular format: music. Incorporeal, volatile, vertical, it allows the spectator to escape reality and truly liberate themselves. Music can transcend the rectangular format to liberate the spectator in the spiritual scope of a verticality that opens. In Ramón Griffero's case horizontally, his dramatic art develops a popular music whose function is to let us hear the people's dreams; but, vertically, this same music makes us realize interior exile as the only lived utopia." Jerome Stephan, *Three Vanguard Theatres: Meyerhold, Fassbinder, Griffero*, Santiago de Chile: Editorial ARCIS, 2011.

> scenes to theatrical scenes and trying to reconfigure the chosen scenes and change their filmic values to a scenic language.
>
> Let's choose one or more sequences from a film and analyze their characters, texts, actions, planes, and sounds. On the basis of the following template, we will structure the film script so that it serves us as a guide for this exercise.
>
> Film Sequence: Text–Actors–Location–Plan–Soundtrack
>
> Amplifying the visuality of the space allows the playwright to liberate themselves from a possible impossibility of performing their writing, by thinking that the stage can't contain it.

It is on the basis of this perception and practice that I have been able to create works like *Your Desires in Fragments*, that take place in different emotional compartments of a mind, allowing us to traverse the broad gamut of temporalities of a thought. In the text of *End of Eclipse* meanwhile, a sequence moves from a scene in the nineteenth century, to a sequence aboard an aircraft carrier invading Iraq, to a situation on a Caribbean beach. In another scene, referring to the coup d'etat, the temporalities and places transpire simultaneously, with the official who receives an order of execution, the pain of the prisoner, his wife walking through the streets, his execution, and the end where both flee aboard a schooner, interacting.

Considering the writing process from the perspective of a Dramaturgy of Space constitutes a motor that opens possibilities for writing and staging, as well as offers the actor the possibility of broadening their interpretive range. A poetics of space created not for its own existence alone conducts us to an artistic gesture that derives from the intangible process of creation. The construction of a poetics of text as much as of images has a strong referential weight with respect to the visual culture where it is inserted, complemented by its own dramatic tradition. I would also say that, today, the poetics of images are engraved in our cultural references more than the sentences of verbal construction. In constructing scenic images, we find ourselves permanently faced with the obstacle of what has already been seen, reused, and, therefore, lacks the power of seduction. Thus, the representation of a girl in a hat with a pink ribbon and a doll, the character wearing a black suit with a suitcase, the actress in a slip and high heels with loose hair, as well as bodies in black mesh bags above water troughs are visually established and exhausted clichés, along with thousands more.

This doesn't signify that their conscious restoration can't establish an artistic, parodic, dramatic citation of these preceding conventions. This text only gives the principles, tools, or conditions to elaborate poetics, but isn't a manual for an automatic result. That will be the product of the creation of the author, group, their sensibility and the necessities they bring to representing or creating spiritual and political worlds that emerge from their imaginary.

# CHAPTER III

## Relationships between a Poetics of Space and the Poetics of a Text

All the exercises described until now are built using codes that can be realized without the presence of a dramatic text. They can be worked with and perceived as a continuity of scenic images.

Nevertheless, the actions proposed in this book have as their objective the introduction of a perspective on the constructions of the subtextual narratives inherent in the space, and, simultaneously, as an approach to the codes of the scenic alphabet that allow us to relate the format with the poetics of the text to be performed, or its writing with its scenic materialization. This process is an elaboration of the union of written thought with the artistic procedures of its visual writing. Such praxis establishes the global concept of The Dramaturgy of Space.

In continuation, I will develop some reflections on my approach to dramatic writing and the craft of the playwright.

## The Dramatic Text as a Construction in Process

The first gesture of the scenic word can be summarized as the decontextualization of an idiom/language, in a fictional place, emitted by a voice. Its least exclamation or sonority already corresponds to the ambit of the dramatic word, it is the abstraction of an idea, an emotion, a discourse, the beginnings of a story.

In the space, the word acquires a value that doesn't refer only to its enunciation, since it doesn't refer to or arise from a "real" present but proposes a symbiosis between the authorial poetics of space and visual constructions of reality, that the spectator lacks prior references for, and that are emitted by a preassigned body. We can illustrate this with the colloquial expression "I don't have sufficient words to express what I feel, or what's happening to me." By means of the theatrical creative gesture we draw from the poetics of space images of emotions and situations that the word fails to enunciate. And it is here that scenic language manifests what can't be embraced, what's not said.

Keeping the concept of The Dramaturgy of Space in mind, we recognize the poetics of the text and the poetics of the space and perceive that each one of these concepts is form and content at once, and it is in the assemblage of all the codes that each one contains: writing, acting, sub dramaturgies, that the final dramatic text is delivered to us.

Seen from this perspective, writing the text is nothing more than a pretext. Writings freed from paradigms and integrated into the universe of scenic creations frame each text as a fragment of perpetual writing. Each performance of a work rewrites it, making appear or disappear the other performances of the text that haven't been constructed. In this way the dramatic text is transformed into a work perpetually under construction, since it is always in a phase previous to that of its constitution as a finished work. This vision facilitates the appearance of the integral author: playwright, director, designer, who we can designate as "playwrights of space."

No text is ontologically conditioned to a form of performance, or to a predetermined poetics of space. If we have a predetermined vision of how to perform a text, it most likely corresponds to the forms used by the previous artistic spirit to perform it, or to the latest visual narrative in vogue.

The possibility that a classical, modern, or postmodern text be performed in authorial form comes from the approaches, readings, and sensibilities that confrontations with this text's narrative cause to appear.

The sum total of performances in theatre history serve as references for the multiple poetics of space that the text has had. Nothing prevents us from citing them, but none of those poetics corresponds to a preestablished concept for its form of performance.

The challenge in constructing the visual narrative of a text is to strengthen its discourse again, reformulate its scenic actions, give it a fictional environment that will reveal the emotions and visions it contains once more. If we perform the character of Prometheus inserted into a wall of screens with bombers attacking him, or as a young rebel, isolated, listening to music, this constitutes the re-elaboration of the image of the situation and state of being the play gives us, and, therefore, takes us to another perspective of its temporality, its action, and the codes that derive from putting it in space. Nothing here prevents the performance's emotional essences from corresponding with the proposed fable.

Playwriting, above all in the twentieth century, developed in such a way that ascribed its texts to forms of representation that corresponded to innovations in the construction of fiction. We understand that artistic discourse, as it resituates itself, changes its storytelling structures to recreate and differentiate fictions, as much from what precedes it, as to a generate a creative gesture related to a spiritual and political vision of the world that was, that invades it, or that it proposes.

Texts don't only deliver a literary story, but also induce forms of performance, which essentially differentiates them from the category of literary work. Dramatic writing, besides proposing a linguistic structure, carries with it, in its construction, a spatial temporal structure, whether as indicated by its stage directions or by the non-written dimensions that construct the story.

In the development of Western Theatre, there are moments when dramatic structures have reformulated or generated the diversification of the visual narratives to be constructed. The dramatic text, to be put onstage, has proposed challenges, producing breaks with previous forms of performance, impelling transformations in scenic language, establishing a dialogue between the poetics of space and the poetics of text, spurring the emergence of other scenic conventions and fictional structures.

A Romantic theatre suggests to us rooms with chimneys, curtains blowing in the wind, candles, balconies and armchairs, chests of memories and read letters. Psychological Realistic writing transforms the scenic concepts from its convention. In the same way that Symbolist texts situate the story in metaphysical spaces and modify the interpretation, suggesting that the word in their texts emerges from the soul of the actor. An Expressionist dramaturgy takes us to the nightmares of a personal journey (*Ich drama*), to the phantoms of war and the cry for existence. To perform the anguishes of existence its visual narrative derives from black and white images and a world of leaning walls that crush us. The dramaturgy of the Theatre of the Absurd, the Theatre of Panic, of a "political" or postmodern theatre, proposes other approaches for the visual narrative of its texts. And some conceptual texts as well, where in the substratum of their words, the scenic atmospheres, corresponding to states of being or mental fictions, challenge the poetics of space to realize their staging.

The poetics of text suggests poetics of space to us, places and visualities inserted in its writing. It proposes mental spaces, atmospheres, structures of action, voices, or characters—a performance language.

This isn't only a question of form, it is intrinsically joined to the premise that if a piece of writing contains a worldview, that must be reflected not only in the text, but also in the reconstruction we make of that vision in the space.

The ways we rewrite the text when we move it to the stage are an essential part of the politics of the theatre. Whoever stages a dramatic text desires to complete that vision in their performance, not for the zeal of creative egocentrism, but from the conviction of an emotional and political impulse, tied to their sensorial reading and reality, and inserted into their territorial frame, which gives meaning to their creation and to the development of scenic language.

The transformations of the visual narrative or the narrative capacities contained in the story through the rectangle, generate the development of dramatic writing in relation to the new capacities generated by the format and vice versa.

Comprehension of the fable through the procedures of narrative fragmentation advance in relation to the ways that scenic temporalities of place or mind are resolved, as proposed by the writing. The unity of action and place that a dramatic text contained at determined moments in history was intimately linked to the imaginative capacities of a particular spatial-temporal conception.

The development of other temporalities in literature, as well as the appearance of film, facilitated the use of temporalities in playwriting as part of its story. The concept of writing for the scenic format, and the development of visual narrative broadened the textual structures and forms of narration in the craft of playwriting.

As an example, Büchner wrote *Woyzeck* in 1836. Its structure of more than thirty scenes, some brief, couldn't be performed until

1913, since the visual narrative that sustained it wasn't within the imaginary of spatial possibilities for performance at the time.

The irruption of the theatre director as organizer of scenic languages onstage reminds us that it is a skill that arises at the end of the nineteenth century, and from its appearance visual narrative begins to have equivalent preponderance to the poetics of text.

During the 1970s and 1980s the role of the director was talked about as the central figure in the process of creation, and thus there was speculation about the disappearance of the playwright. Directors fragmented texts and developed their own poetics of space contributing to the development of the scenic alphabet, in a moment that made the visual predominate the verbal.

This phenomenon of visual language acquired preponderance in a context culturally dominated by the power of the image and as the motor and sign of performance. The spectacular dimension comes to predominate the analysis of a work and consolidates the scenic stamp of an era.

Within the ambit of theatrical work, the preceding can be explained by a void in dramaturgical scenic proposals, since the existing writings corresponded to or were associated with a poetics of space that didn't respond to the urgencies or necessities of those new directors. Thus, in the face of an absence of texts linked to the development of the visuality of the stage, the director assumes the text as pretext for their own poetics, in a practice centered on the development of visual narratives as the place closest to their vision of the world. This certainly contributed to a great development in scenic visual language, in the narrative capacities of the body, light, objects, and the use of non-theatrical spaces as places for the work.

The emergence of so-called contemporary writings, a process in which playwrights return to positioning the text as writing that carries visualities with it and isn't limited by closed spatial concepts, generates a resurgence of the theatrical text, now connected to new conceptions of performance. We could say that during those years, the director's craft elaborated new visual narratives that were later reincorporated into dramatic writings, and that have allowed a re-reading of texts from our dramatic patrimony. Thus, the previous exercise allowed a return to a relationship with the playwriting tradition from an authorial perspective.

This phenomenon led to a profusion of director-playwrights (or vice versa), since their concepts of writing developed intimately linked to a conception of the poetics of space that they wanted to manifest, and without which the text would not acquire a prefigured political and artistic reading, since their writing contained a scenic visuality, typologies of acting, designs, and views about the environment they wanted to materialize.

In this frame The Dramaturgy of Space, in its broadest meaning, emerges from a unified vision.

# The Impossibility of Speaking Like Writing

One of the motors for why people write is the communicative schizophrenia of thoughts, emotions, and visions that don't find a way to manifest themselves in daily social dimension. We can't greet someone saying, "Good morning, your eyes remind me of a valley of bleeding olives." Our daily verbal structure doesn't accede to, nor is socially appropriate for, manifesting our feelings in this manner. It doesn't correspond to daily speech, nor can our imaginative lexicon emit sentences that elaborate the psychic dimension of thought and its emotions. Were it to happen, it would appear contextually inappropriate, and wouldn't be heard or felt as a form of our cultural expression within a recognizable context.

Writing, at the instant of its creation, liberates words from their context and lets the playwright appropriate them and give them signs or visualizations or connotations that he structures. Thus, phrases not said, texts elaborated and inserted into a poetics constitute the idiom of theatricality. The enunciation of dramatic texts onstage is the space and product of one of the magics of performance. The actor or actress can speak like writing, manifesting what is hidden in a thought, or our sensory constructions. Allowing by means of the word, the reconstruction of the signs and visualities of our idiom in order to transmit ideas that social language doesn't usually contain.

This is one of the difficulties for an actor in appropriating a text, speaking it as it is written, without revealing that it is the written word. This appropriation is where one of the strengths of the dramatic text and its interpretation is sustained.

The language of writing is constructed by restructuring the idiom to which we subscribe, reinventing, re-elaborating words and phrases, allowing a more emotional relationship between situation and verb. An action that allows the establishment of a textual intimacy with the spectator, such that words go beyond their condition of expressions already constituted or external, to also become part of the spectator's internal dialogue, producing an emotional resonance in the spectator's psyche, so that they leave their condition of listener behind and become a participant in the action.

## Our Emotions Are Mute: The Theatre Gives Them Voice

As can be deduced from the preceding, scenic writing, like all literary expression in its textual poetics, gives to emotions, words, and phrases that are mute in their realistic context.

We feel pain, our states of love, of impotence, of existential reflection, or discomfort faced with an environment, but we don't verbally elaborate the amplitude of sensations hidden by those moments. We don't exclaim a monologue in the face of situations of happiness or anguish; at weddings, funerals, depressions, declarations of love, our social phrases are brief or formally preestablished.

The playwright rebuilds words, the names of our emotions and our internal states. Verbalizing in this way the pain a mother feels at her son's death or bringing to life the thought of a man confronting the universe. They give phrases to internal thought and voices to the lives of our emotions.

The playwright constructs these soliloquies, silences, unspoken dialogues and gives them life. The listener identifies their emotion with the text emitted. Thus, the emotions are no longer mute, and the writer has the difficult mission of transforming them into verbal expression of thoughts as powerful as the actions from which they arise.

Our sentences should be as strong as the actions they represent, and the theatrical actions they represent should be, at the same time, as strong as the textual poetics they sustain. This doesn't prevent clichéd dialogue or exclamations in the face of emotional situations from also being part of a dramatic text, which from that basis searches for a way to reveal the iconography of our idiom, or the formation of our linguistic expressions and their correspondence with the discourses valued by the social structures of the dominant hegemonic fiction.

## What is Named Exists, or, the Empowerment of Knowledge

By naming it the author makes what one can't see exist onstage, be it an external or internal place, at the same time bringing relationships, conflicts, and knowledge into existence. The actor can say "This foggy night bewilders me," and we know in this way where they are speaking from. "Come closer to the precipice," "Let's get off this boat," "The city is burning," "The sky darkens."

Words make visible what the stage still doesn't reveal. Like the poetics of space make visible what words hide.

And they also signal the hierarchical condition of who is onstage, their relationship or their internal conflict. "What are you doing to her, my king?" "I always hated being your father." "I am god of the sea." Besides naming the actions that happen, are going to happen, or have happened, from the different temporalities of the idiom.

If the preceding is inherent in the most anecdotal of dramatic writing, the most relevant point, and one that, perhaps, is not always realized, is that in the construction of fictions and stories we don't only use the memories of our our inheritance and imaginaries given to us by the world in which we arrive. In addition, a text's challenge is to succeed, by means of its discourses and actions, in amplifying or constructing other forms of knowledge.

Renaissance theatre gave voice and prominence to the individual, proposing them as the artificer of their own actions and divorced from the divine ideology of the Middle Ages. It laid the foundation for a way of thinking that envisioned that power and self-determination were born with the individual. This created an opening for the gestation of the ideas elaborated by modern fiction and democracy.

It is important to underscore that the fictions of art, as much in performance as in dramatic writing, construct ideas and fictions that will later assume their place in reality. They will contribute to its development and will be incorporated into its dimension, whether in actuality or desire.

As we approach contemporary writing, we can't always elucidate the meaning or implications of a text, nor of the fables to which it refers. What we do know is that these texts are generated by our own species, that scrutinize the essences of our existence and reveal our desires. When we elaborate ideas and construct stories, we make them exist and strengthen the politics of writing.

## Writing and Social Linguistic Structures

We use our own language in a text, which carries with it a linguistic history and a verbal structure of transmission of thought and emotions. Language is an instrument of social cohabitation, ideological transmission, and the construction of power. It operates in our individual relationships as much as in our social relations, and in the globalized world. This means that, beyond the fable narrated the manner of relation is essential. We have to be able to distinguish when the language used cites, deconstructs, or creates, or employs other linguistic schemes to transmit the views or intentions of that fable.

Discourses of power carry with them a total summary of common places. They appear as the official or dissident form of communication and evolve to establish themselves as contemporaneous expression.

Institutions reinvent their phrases, their allocutions, and the form in which they inculcate us through education, social mediums, or influences. They structure our thoughts or give us phrases, turning us into verbal transmitters of the values, ideas, and views of the preestablished culture, causing us to constantly repeat those ideas. The religious person will refer to their faith, in the same way that their "mystic" authorities refer to it. A member of a political party will refer to reality by reiterating the discourses shared with their "political class." The managerial structure will speak from its business vocabulary and its managers, employees themselves, will repeat these discourses. Advertising discourses, whether from showbusiness or global phrases and forms of communication like those constructed for the virtual world (Facebook, Twitter, SMS) are linguistic structures that allow us to feel part of a market culture, a subculture, or part of an antisystemic nucleus. Social classes will ascribe their idiomatic expressions to their emotions and use forms of social communication in accord with the class they are linked to or wish to join. Nationalities, juvenile groups, sects, ethnic minorities or majorities, academics, or sexualities speak and distinguish themselves through forms of linguistic construction related to their identity.

The role of institutions, identity, and language in the construction of our social structure is already over-studied. The purpose of this recounting is to understand, develop, and consider the role our linguistics occupy within the poetics of a text.

The decontextualization of social discourses in the scenic space allows the revelation of social linguistic structures. By abstracting them from their surroundings and situating them in the fiction of art, we can view them critically. At the same time, the playwright in their plays can disseminate, consecrate, and perpetuate socialized discourses and shape the scenic representation of them. They can also relate to them with a textual poetics, as much from their references to dramaturgical tradition, as from constructing other discourses that confront the fiction of existing discourses, deepening the mechanism of the decontextualization of the word and the autonomy of scenic language.

# The Tradition of Dramatic Language as Reference for Contemporary Writings

All of the linguistic and dramatic structures of preceding periods, their forms of constructing phrases, dialogues, and developing fables are today, in their historical decontextualization and in the deconstruction of their original paradigm, material from our inheritance and scenic memory available to be integrated into dramatic writings. In this way we cite the influence of those forms of dramatic construction. This confirms that there is a history of scenic writing for the theatrical forms of the word in each dramatic style: the theatricalized language makes an actor speak in verse, transforming this construction into an idiomatic reality belonging to the stage.

Verse, romantic prose, rhyme, the idiomatic form of construction of ideas and emotions in realistic theatre, agit-prop theatre, symbolist, expressionist, and *costumbrista* theatre can be material for contemporary playwriting. Today's playwright draws upon their contributions for visualizing time and space and creating forms of writing.

For the creation of a contemporary textual poetics, all previous dramatic structures used to construct fables are codes that feed and nourish a dramaturgy that re-elaborates or integrates preceding linguistic dramatic structures, generating a new decontextualization of these expressions and, therefore, other readings.

# Of the Appropriation of a Text

Texts are the means by which an idea and the emotions that it causes or inspires are developed. Texts cause us to see what is happening in the body, the truth or falsity of what the speaker has to perform.

The textual resonances in the body reflect the intimacy of its being, its vision of what is happening. They will make us realize its submission to power, love, or a system. They will signal a nonexistent being in our environment, an angel, someone from the beyond or some parallel dimension. The body's speech constitutes it and, if the performer appropriates it, incarnates it. He speaks and not the text. It is a fictional body and not a reproducer of phrases.

A performer gives the text breath and texture. By placing the daily inflections of grammar within the context of emotion and scenic actions the performer can exceed or surpass them and a new way of speaking emerges.

Since the morphology of the cultural expression of emotion varies in its representation according to different historical periods, bodily interpretation of the text is in consonance with acting language that reflects the spirit of the age.

The modes of interpreting emotion and its corporeal signs are referred to in the historical development of the actor's art, in the same way that the scenic actions an actor executed corresponded to the conventions elaborated in each period. The construction of the word to express love has a writing and scenic action corresponding to the forms of love in its period and the moral and conventional limitations in performing it. Lovers in classical theatre suggest sexual desire through subtext, but it wasn't physically demonstrated in the staging of their time.

We ascribe typologies of interpretation (characters, icons, speakers) and scenic actions (conceptual, plastic, abstract, functional) to the word according to the language we develop, according to the reading we make of the text. Thus, a text as common, as simple, as: "Caballito blanco, llévame de aquí llévame a mi pueblo donde nací" (Little white horse, take me away from here, take me to the town where I was born) becomes a fundamental text when inserted into the context of a scene, where the situation it relates valorizes and produces theatrical actions that give dramatic force to a structure as basic as that described. If the character speaking that text is murmuring to his dead son it acquires a tragic tone, but it would carry the feeling of a thriller if, in another scene, he sang while strangling his victim, or turn dark if the text is delivered by a torturer in action. "Little white horse" could also be the great final love song of a musical, demonstrating how a theatrical text's signification is infinitely changeable depending upon the visuality of the action. The dramatic text, according to the scenic situation in which it is immersed, will be transformed and produce different results.

In this case it will be the poetics of space, (the action to be realized and the situation where it arises) that is to say, the subtext of that text and not the word itself, that will open its understanding to us.

We also have the option of annulling the original fiction of a text through the staging or the place where it is spoken, attributing another fictional convention to the original text. An actor who, in the midst of his acting, takes out the text and reads it, or a staging that recreates the study of the text, shows us rehearsal and the process of construction, gives us a work in progress. Other examples are inflections and separation of words marking a performative action that wants to make the vowels stand out, singing the dialogue with a musical group, or any other possibility seen or imagined for the stage.

In this way we can see a profound symbiosis between the poetics of space and the poetics of text in theatrical creation. That symbiosis establishes the convention used, given that each textual poetics can be linked to infinite forms of performance, reiterating one of the premises of The Dramaturgy of Space.

All dramatic texts were written to perform a fiction onstage, transmuting the space into the fable's universe. An imaginary world is visualized, translated into planes and actions, situations and conflicts. It paints the spirit of the age, speaks to us of the species, from the labyrinth of its emotions. All of this forms the incomprehensibility of life and death and the kindnesses and atrocities of our actions.

Writing is destined for an infinite space, that, when named, we show. This space can contain all times, all histories, in multiple dimensions. The visual narrative that gives life and existence to a textual poetics is unlimited in its ability to contain thought.

# CHAPTER IV

*I adore fictional bullets because they have never stained the stage with blood.*

FIN DE ECLIPSE

## Dramaturgy of Space in Scenic Practice

In this section I will establish a relationship between the concepts expressed so far in the book and their application in a selection of plays written between 1984 and 2007. A scenic practice that crosses different historical dimensions. I call them dimensions because of the profound changes in the spirit of the age during those times, beginning during the Cold War and the Chilean dictatorship, crossing the democratic transition, and facing globalization today.

I will not enter into a self-analysis of the fables' structures. Better to turn our attention to an emphasis on underlining how diverse texts, in their dramatic structures, relate to different conceptualizations of the spatial narrative, and how this was perceived by different theatre researchers, academics, and critics.

The selection considers the relationships between poetics of text and space, for which we propose the following three categories.

## A) Poetics of Text and Space/Place

*Historias de un Galpón Abandonado* (*Stories From an Abandoned Warehouse*) (1984)
*Cinema Utoppia* (1985)
*99 La Morgue* (1986)
*Río Abajo* (*Downstream*) (1995)

## B) Visual Productions of the Poetics of Abstract Space

*Santiago Bauhaus* (1987)
*Azar de la Fiesta* (*Luck of the Draw*) (1992)

## C) Textual Poetics—Conceptual Spaces

*Brunch o Almuerzos de Mediodía* (*Brunch or Petit Dejeuner du Midi*) (1999)
*Tus Deseos en Fragmentos* (*Your Desires in Fragments*) (2003)
*Fin de Eclipse* (*End of the Eclipse*) (2007)

# Poetics of Text and Space/Place

The fictional space of these four plays references the personal experiences, pains, and resistance of a country under dictatorship and in transition. They are transformed into actions that occur in urban-social places that resonated with me as metaphors for moments of an historical condition.

As the desolated, isolated inhabitants of a warehouse in *Historias de un Galpón Abandonado*. As spectators and actors in a film we can't comprehend in *Cinema Utoppia*. Forming part of a country transformed into a morgue in *99 La Morgue*. And from the forced cohabitation of memory and the present in a building on the banks of a river in *Río Abajo*.

## *Historias de un Galpon Abandonado*—1984

This play's title references the idea of being immersed in a large space, a place without exits. The characters arrive carrying the residues of their lives and personal experiences with them, inhabit the space, are subjected to abuse, and given false hopes by those who dominate the warehouse. They do so from an immense baroque wardrobe, territory of power, morality, and wealth, in direct opposition to the state of its inhabitants.

"El Trolley" (1984–8) was inaugurated with this play as a creative space for Teatro Fin de Siglo and an artistic space of resistance to the dictatorship. As such it brought together innumerable artistic expressions of dance, music, theatre, video art, installations, and literature, as well as concerts, parties, and events during its existence.

The creators who showed their work in this space became a fundamental part of the cultural renovation of the country.

El Trolley's entire warehouse was used to create the show's atmosphere. The play's initial stage directions already signal concepts relating to the poetics of the body, the use of the space, and the dramaturgy of the object:

*Indications for the movements and spatial situations of the characters are only outlines from which you should work, since the staging centers on the atmospheric creation. Each character's spatial position, their constant or erratic movements, their mimicry, form a slow choreographic evolution. So you should always take into account that while characters are speaking in a situation, the activities of the other inhabitants of the warehouse continue around them according to the play's dramatic evolution. The inhabitants of this warehouse aren't "psychological" characters in the dogmatic theatrical sense, but synthesized characters, and the interpreter is asked to constantly exacerbate their emotions, mark each situation with the greatest possible force, consciously and graphically manipulate objects. The play is a metaphor, the actors and objects are part of it.*

Agustín Letelier, an academic and theatre critic who attended the first performances of this production and of the work presented there, gives us his vision:

At a time of social tension, its transgressive positions could be interpreted as centrally political but, in reality, its audience followed it in a more integral form. At the end of performances at the warehouse El Trolley, near Mapocho Station (it was an unthinkable place for attracting a theatre audience), people didn't leave. They stayed for a party in which the transgressive climate was shown in the clothing, conversations, the groups that formed, and the intellectual effervescence breathed.

Ramón Griffero's work is characterized by what he has called "dramaturgy of space", a term that alludes to a wide range of significations. The impact he achieved with *Historias de un Galpón Abandonado* in 1984 came, in great measure, from the series of surprises produced throughout the performance. To begin with, the place selected was effectively a partially abandoned warehouse that was almost completely occupied as a stage. A quantity of heterogeneous objects—chairs of different types, beds, tables—were disseminated in this wide space, that ended in a large wardrobe with three doors. What seemed to be a decoration became another scenic space from which characters came and went. When the three doors were finally opened, another complete stage appeared. This game of surprise with the appearance of new places showed a distinct conception of performance and theatrical space.

(*Diario El Mercurio*, 1984)

PHOTOGRAPH 1 *Historias de un Galpón Abandonado.*

CHAPTER IV 137

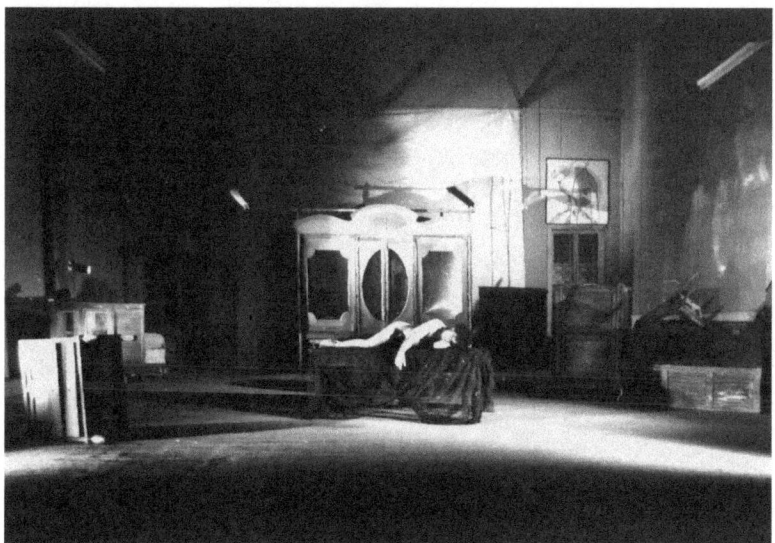

**PHOTOGRAPH 2** *Historias de un Galpón Abandonado.*

## *Cinema Utoppia*—1985

### The juxtaposition of spatial temporal dimensions and the cinematification of the stage

Set in 1946, the play takes place in the Teatro Valencia, where seven solitary characters attend the last performance before the movie theatre closes. Seated in the theatre they watch the screen absorbed by the story set in the future of a young Chilean exiled in France in the 1980s, living with the memory of a failed utopia and of his girlfriend detained and disappeared, officially anonymous. Dressed in their best clothes, this group of eccentric strangers, including the usher who has never left the theatre, an old maid with depressive tendencies, an old man never separated from the rabbit he keeps as a good luck charm, and a young man with Down's Syndrome, come day after day to see the same film: *Utoppia*. In this strange way they confront the future politics of their territory.

The play takes place on three overlapping spatial temporal planes. To configure the fable the narrative levels in relation to

PHOTOGRAPH 3 *Cinema Utoppia.*

the space are articulated in perspective: as three scenic rectangles that, in their interaction, produce the fiction's narration of different spatial temporal dimensions. Those three rectangles are at the same time inserted into the general rectangle of the scenic format.

These spaces are presented in the following manner:

*First rectangle:*
The general frame of the play: a movie theatre in 1946, orchestra, seats, access doors.
*Second rectangle:*
The movie screen. An interior, a room. The story of young exiles in France in 1980.
*Third rectangle:*
Within the room, a window giving out on to a street and a telephone booth, framing the action that takes place beyond it.

The juxtaposition of these rectangles in a line creates a sense of depth. Each place contains at the same time its own temporal dimensions, the phantoms of the disappeared in the theatre, scenes of simultaneous past and present, what takes place inside the screen, and the narrative interaction of the "film-scene" and the theatre space. The protagonists of the film leave the screen to console the usher, or in the final scene, the spectators from the Valencia movie theatre appear as characters integrated into the film *Utoppia*.

**PHOTOGRAPH 4** *Cinema Utoppia.*

**PHOTOGRAPH 5** *Cinema Utoppia.*

The cinematification of the stage isn't only applied to the theatrical sequence that takes place on the screen and that should create the convention of a projected film, but also in the narrative of the text, of the actor's composition, the framed planes, ellipses, which all refer what we see visually to a recognizable cinematographic style. At the same time, there are several sequences where the narration is sustained in the moving image supported by a soundtrack that gives support to the scenic actions, an effect that reinforces the convention of a cinematified theatrical scene.

The theorist and academic Dr. Alfonso de Toro realized how this visual narrative is perceived:

> The dramatic text is divided into four days, but its performance syntax is obviously determined by the alteration of the two fundamental planes already mentioned, that of the movie theatre the audience attends to see a film titled "Utoppia" (first part), and the film scene itself that develops in a room. The window of this room opens on to another space: the street, that is superimposed as a third space. As a fourth space we should include that of the spectators in the theatre. Thus, we have two types of superimpositions: one in which the real spectators see the same work as the actor-spectators and another that is the reproduction of performance experience, that is to say, the duplication of the spectator. Within the projected film, Esteban films a movie: with this we have a duplication of the filmmaker's activity and a triplication of the play as a theatrical work, as film, and as film within film. In this way the action transcends a merely anecdotal state and acquires a meta-spectacular function. Griffero is talking to us about the terror and consequences of the dictatorship, but at the same time is discovering for us the labor of "making theatre", putting the naked "spectacular artifact" in front of us. Thus, Griffero surpasses the spectator's mere identification with a determined content by revealing his theatrical processes, impelling the spectator into a dialogue with form and with their condition now when confronted with the condition of those from then within the frame of the dictatorship. Through this process, Griffero incorporates two aspects that in Latin American Theatre, in general, are divided.
> 
> (Alfonso de Toro, *Teatro Fin de Siglo—El Trolley*, Santiago de Chile: Neptuno Editores, 1992)

Theatre researcher and critic Juan Andrés Piña for his part points out:

> The premiere of *Cinema Utoppia* was a determining factor in the renovation of the national stage. One that searched for aspects of an expressive mode that belonged more to the stage, rather than to the word or the dialogue to capture the sensibility of the period. Exploring diverse theatrical spaces, the potentialities of scenography and lighting, of new scenic idioms that moved away from traditional conversations, Griffero's proposal was also a way to show us themes of hidden Chileanness or, as was definitively present, the marginality of those years: exile, drug addiction, the destruction of ideas and people and all that the system left outside. A generation of directors grew in parallel with and in relation to Griffero and became innovators of the Chilean stage, an inheritance lasting until today. The Belgian scene designer Herbert Jonckers' (1954–1996) work was decisive in connecting theatrical, architectonic, and kinetic codes. He impelled a spatial aesthetic that others imitated with disparate results.
>
> (Juan Andrés Piña, *20 años de teatro chileno*, Santiago de Chile: Editorial Ril, 1998)

**PHOTOGRAPH 6** *Cinema Utoppia.*

## 99 La Morgue—1987

A multidimensional text and the fragmentation of the scenic rectangle

The spirit of this play is expressed in its stage directions:

> *Because you had to run through the streets and the funerals thinking about how that newly fallen one, martyr of an afternoon, would hear from inside his urn so many shouts, hear himself called present so many times, and there were already so many first names and surnames. Because silent funerals no longer existed as if you no longer died for yourself, but for something.*
>
> *Thinking about what the frozen autopsy table would feel like and of wanting to have been able to live a minute more, to say that you had watched out for this precise moment.*
>
> *And those precise moments inhabited the future and the past but never the present. And because thought fails to trap an idea anymore, or please itself with any, and because images seem to be the philosophy of these years, and for the pleasure of seeing those philosophies on the stage, and for the pleasure of destroying its images.*

Thus we arrived at this text's first stage directions, filling it with images without name, of thoughts without verb. It is a textual puzzle of multiple dimensions, joined together by the logic of associations, that can carry the spectator's imagination to infinity, or to the end of our capacity to perform.

*99 La Morgue* deals with the well-known problem produced by dictatorships, when the forensic doctors declare those assassinated by the police or tortured to be accidental or natural deaths (cardiac arrests, deficiencies of whatever type). The staging and its content should be analyzed and interpreted considering the fact that to perform this play even while Pinochet was still in power, signified a risk as much for the author as for the director and actors. It was something serious and an extremely dangerous reality.

### The Space and Scenic Time

The show has a central space, the room in the morgue, that is divided into several subspaces. In front of the spectator can be

PHOTOGRAPH 7 *99 La Morgue.*

found the large enclosure surrounded by green walls. In the part at the back of the raised platform, behind the sliding doors, is an elevated platform with the table where the autopsies are carried out. This same is transformed at times into a dais where *entremeses* from the sixteenth and eighteenth centuries are performed. To its right, behind folding doors in a kind of showcase window, is Germán's mother's room in the whorehouse, then a hall, and Germán's room where he dedicates himself to painting in his free moments.

These spaces alternate, intentionally reoccurring. The central scenes in the morgue (with cadavers to be examined or scenes of torture) are interrupted by scenes of dialogue between Germán and Fernanda and memories from the past: Fernanda and her evangelical childhood, Germán and his childhood with his mother, scenes from the entremeses, or scenes in which the Director takes on the roles of the Roman Emperor or of Lady Macbeth; and scenes of the grandmother in her role as Corintio's wife. While the scenes in the morgue play out in the immediate present, the others are performed in diverse pasts. This technique, which we also found in *Cinema Utoppia*, has the pragmatic function of removing the discourse and its highly veiled message from *hic et nunc*, which represents an evident danger in the face of the ruling political circumstances. It is linked to the dramaturgical goal of filling the ethical void in the discourse of the morgue's director. The story of the Alvarez sisters is a mirror of the morgue that thematizes the problem of repression, confinement, arbitrariness and the negation of the other. This discourse is equivalent to that of the director in the present who cynically proclaims the ethical purposes of his profession, which has been transformed into a criminal instrument of repression, and that allows the morgue to function as an infernal house of death. Griffero employs the spatial-temporal dimension resulting in an extra-theatrical situation, but with a dramaturgical purpose that contributes to the insinuation of the hidden throughout the principal scenes by deterritorializing the message, to then remake it into another code.

(Alfonso de Toro, *Teatro Fin de Siglo—El Trolley*,
Santiago de Chile: Neptuno Editores, 1992)

## *Río Abajo*—1995

### Verticality and superimposition of the scenic rectangle

*Río Abajo* is part of a series of plays that emerge from an urban symbolic place. The play takes place in a three-story building located in the urban periphery of Santiago, on the banks of the Mapocho River. This river leaves the mountain range, above the city, first crossing the affluent neighborhoods, then leaving the city and crossing through the more marginal neighborhoods, which is where the name of the play comes from.

It is a metaphor for our period of democratic transition, where in this building/country the residues of the social pain of the dictatorship must live together. The wife of a man detained and disappeared lives next to an ex-torturer now dedicated to drug dealing, along with the generation that has inherited this social situation—one in which torturers' children live side by side with the children of the disappeared. Among them are a gay young man and a girl discriminated against because she is fat, characters that the new democracy prefers to forget, erase from recent memory.

This building allows the fusion of the collective with the individual by means of an X-ray of the lives of each of its inhabitants. Those who have survived and who re-elaborated the faults of the past cohabit there with those who the new political order considers unnecessary, next to the illusions of the 1990s youth brimming with ideals in the midst of a country where only those upriver prosper.

> Above all, I am grateful that *Río Abajo* is built on a perception of reality that gives a face to the problems being lived in Chile. One that is affirmed in the expressive will of a playwright who has something to say, who has observed, who has lived, who dares to affirm, who can bring to light from his point of view an investigation of the pain that, like a bad conscience, has injured our life: the helplessness with which we are left once they have undermined all of our moral fortresses. The impossibility for the characters of transcending their own circumstances, the permanent delirium and alienation in which they live, the game of projections and of necessities that one and another try to satisfy, the perversion of domination, the incapacity of living love, the urgency of desire as the only space of closeness but never of giving, are the expression of a human interchange exposed without concessions, solemn in its brutality.
> (Inés Margarita Sanger, "Un disparo al corazon (A shot to the heart)," *Revista Apuntes* No. 110)

*Río Abajo* is centered on a spatial narrative that interacts with the different rectangular spaces that construct the story. We have the superimposition of nine rectangles, six apartments, and three spaces in the staircase corridor, plus the general rectangle of the stage that contains this building, plus the banks of the river.

The story is structured by ellipses, simultaneous past and present, constant parallel scenes, global situations that involve the entire building as individual actions, plus the situations that take place on the banks of the river with the building in back. The subdivision of the geometric space of the stage, the production design, and the cinematographic narrative arise as base and foundation for the elaboration of a dramatic text.

PHOTOGRAPH 8  *Río Abajo.*

The general principal was not to realize a literal reproduction of this block of apartments, but a plastic sculpture of them. The rectangular superimposition produces a composition that reminds us of a giant screen formed by multiple individual screens.

While the text references the structure of a cinematographic script, the theatre doesn't allow jump cuts—a character on the third floor of the building can't immediately appear on the bank of the river. Thus, in writing this play, given the multi-parallelism of its actions, it was necessary first to construct the maquette of the building, and from that elaborate the textual puzzle, allowing the spatial narrative in relation to the writing to unify and create the story's continuity. The maquette allowed situating the dramatic actions, as much partial/individual as global/collective, and to visualize when a character spoke a text on one level of the building and the scenic action continued, while meanwhile, in another space another action created the necessary displacements to forge diverse situations.

This juxtaposition of spaces and temporalities and subdivisions is an inverse structure to that of *Cinema Utoppia*, where the spatiality in relation to the writing is produced by means of a depth of field. In *Río Abajo* it is structured in a vertical manner.

> Griffero astutely affirms that he unites a scenic dramaturgy: spaces, objects and costuming, actions and non-verbal behaviors, music, sound, and lighting are imagined by him at the moment of writing and then actualized in the staging creating a unified expression that constitutes the total language of the work. In *99 La Morgue*, the straight, hard lines of the autopsy tables, the white sheets, the aprons and nude or semi-nude bodies confronted us with the unconcealable coldness of death and the unreal spaces of alienation, where volumes, colors, sounds, proportions, lose their daily dimensions. The pure geometric lines that bodies and objects form with their balances and counterbalances, are broken by capricious elements that introduce the coloring and evocations of cabaret. A plastic imaginary performed with playfulness and character. In *Río Abajo*, Griffero plays again with the multiplication of spaces relative to different levels of reality: there are private spaces, different for each character, corresponding to their rooms in a three-story apartment block (in an Italianate theatre, the solution for expansion is in height); the spaces for collective use and semi-public—the staircases and hall;—as well as the public spaces—like the street in front with its telephone and its kiosk-grocery store. Beyond all this, that is to say, closer to the spectators, is the space of intimacy, of emotional complicity, of dreams and confidences, of the subjective and the extra-social, close to nature and the transcendental: is the riverbank.
>
> (María de la Luz Hurtado, "El teatro de Ramón Griffero," *Revista Apuntes* No. 110)

PHOTOGRAPH 9  *Río Abajo.*

# Visual Productions of the Poetics of Abstract Space
## *Santiago Bauhaus*—1987

The abstract space

The production of *Santiago Bauhaus* was structured in a way similar to the actions described in this book and was an homage to the scenic conceptions of Oscar Schlemmer. Its spatial design was the vertical lines of the scenic rectangle and upstage three constructions, representing a circle, a triangle, and a rectangle that, when turned, made three small installations appear.

The spatial sequences began with choreographies of bodies in relation to their focal points and their axes, revealing their relationship with the spatial geometry. Another series centered on corporeal compositions, organic, graphic, and scenic actions; then compositions of plastic and geometric objects and conceptual scenic actions were incorporated. This ended with a citation of the triadic ballet of the Bauhaus and its annihilation by the arrival of Fascism. Other sequences read abstractly referred to the executions of the dictatorship.

The integrated design by Herbert Jonckers articulated a performance consisting of body, sound, and color that develop conceptual abstract images. These are the fundamental basis of the show.

> It isn't a matter of a theatrical work, or a declaration of theoretical foundations. In more than an hour, the playwright makes us take note of an aesthetic of beautiful content in the simple and the elemental: primary colors, pure geometric forms, basic movements. The spectator can immerse themselves in the disconcertion or perplexity produced by the repetition of robotized movements, on the triangles, circles, and lines of the stage. And only when the sense of humor in this parody and sensualized "latinidad" emerges does the spectator relax, enters into the complicit game, begins to read the lips, intentions and subtexts implicit in this show.
> (Luisa Ulibarri, "*Santiago Bauhaus* 1987," *Diario la Época*, Santiago, Chile)

PHOTOGRAPH 10 *Santiago Bauhaus.*

*Santiago Bauhaus* is plastic theatre in the strictest sense. Bringing it to the stage and giving corporeality to movement and the study of forms. The forms reproduced by the play correspond to the aesthetic of Cubism and abstract art, that had greater force twenty or thirty years ago, but whose transfer to the theatre and the coherence of its scenic formulation are of today. Ramón Griffero and his team of actors and technicians have made an "art action" previously reserved for the plastic arts, but now with valid application in the theatre.

(Agustín Letelier, "*Santiago Bauhaus*," *Diario El Mercurio*, 1987)

PHOTOGRAPH 11 *El Azar de la Fiesta.*

# *El Azar de la Fiesta*—1992

False perspective and a conceptual spatial dramaturgy

Motivated by a celebration at the Vicente Huidobro Foundation, this creation was realized as an homage to the poet. The work was structured in sequences of images based on some poems relating to the author's themes and manifestos: the sea, love, war, death. The production took place in the Museum of Natural History in Santiago. Its large architectonic rectangular hall was chosen as the performance space, and the audience was situated on the second floor, around the railing that encloses that place.

Thus, the production's point of view was situated from above and the spatial work composed in relation to the visual angle of the spectator at the zenith of the space. In the middle of this hall is displayed a whale's skeleton, which was incorporated as the large conceptual object of the production. Each sequence of body, object, and music induced diverse compositions and perspectives of the construction and the scenic action.

The bodily actions that took place on the floor had as their function to create the illusion of a depth of field on the floor, like a false perspective. Bodies were composed simulating being in vertical position, on chairs, standing on them, or dancing lying on the surface. During the scene at sea, they were situated behind a ship's rail, others brought blue rectangles on which they swam. In the war scene, the objects were large vertical lines with lightbulbs creating an aerial view of bombed cities.

At the same time we worked with the deconstruction of the body: in one sequence the interpreters wrapped themselves in large solid cylinders that turned in the space like autonomous forms. In another they put their heads into large trays covered in grass and flowers. The audience's vision was of cylinders turning in the hall and of cut-off heads emerging from a garden. Some poems were diagrammed on the floor to be read from above, generating in all an essentially visual poetics of space that was in constant transformation.

PHOTOGRAPH 12 *El Azar de la Fiesta.*

# CHAPTER IV

PHOTOGRAPH 13  *El Azar de la Fiesta.*

# Textual Poetics—Conceptual Spaces
## *Almuerzos de Mediodia o Brunch*—1999

### The infinity of the rectangular space

Writing from the personal experiences of a detained disappeared on the eve of his execution paints a portrait of an experience unlived, without witnesses or story. It also talks about who imposes a sentence of condemnation, through which they themselves become condemned. Laying bare how the illegality of this act becomes the most refined of legalities is also to talk about all the condemned, who, by means of the word, transformed their ideas into actions considered subversive.

The play suggests physical and mental spaces. It is a text of internal soliloquies, of dialogues that unchain thoughts that are verbalized. The protagonist writes the work being performed and at the same time writes another work within this story.

The play talks of death from life, the only possible place to do so. Esteban is condemned to exist, to which is added the double

PHOTOGRAPH 14 *Almuerzos de Mediodía o Brunch.*

condemnation of being a prisoner condemned for his thought and is then also the figure of a detained disappeared. One who will have no trial, nor know when or how he will die, not be able to say goodbye, who knows that his face won't last in memory. This isn't a dramatic fiction, but a form of elimination instituted by a continent.

## The Space of *Midday Lunches*

The text's stage directions indicate the place of action as an infinite space, limited by the large narrow fishbowls that surround the actors: in each of them, a salmon. This establishes general indications for a conceptual poetics of space. The configuration of an abstract space is signaled in this way, proposing the difficulty of creating an infinite place on the stage. The challenge assumed by scene designer Rodrigo Basáez to generate this infinite space was resolved by dividing the stage with three walls of mirrored glass as the back wall.

1) In front of the glass he conceived of an installation that referred to a place of imprisonment of a technological character. Two rows of loudspeakers framed the place from which the protagonist was harassed by noises and voices, plus two metallic benches. Beneath one of them, an aquarium making reference to the fishbowls that surrounded the actors.

2) Behind the central mirror—which turned transparent according to the needs of the composition—the same scenery as the first plane was reproduced. This implied doubling the characters with other actors.

   The concept was to suggest that this first situation was reiterated at times parallel to, and at others different from, the original situation. This space, at the same time, had upstage another glass/mirror and behind it other situations were generated, producing in this way an infinite game of planes.

3) The opaque glass allowed at the same time the realization of scene changes unseen by the spectator, as a means by which to make characters vanish and merge, achieving by this mechanism a deepening in the continuity of a work of scenic cinematification.

In this way, by means of the multiplication of the scenic image realized through the effects of the superimposition/translucency of the mirrors (and the repetition of the scenery), a sense that the scenic image extended into infinity was achieved. By these means we succeeded in putting the stage direction: "In an infinite place" onstage.

The cultural theorist and essayist Nelly Richard deepens and gives us some reflections on this scenic installation:

> First, one must highlight the significant protagonism of the mirrors that function like a critical and formal device whose mechanisms put into play and question the problem of theatrical representation and the artifice of its signs. Griffero has been very insistent (as much in his reflections about the theatre as in his own theatrical creation) on making use of scenic artifices that install a game of distances and cuts, of interruptions, of fragmentations, and of dislocations, in order to subject the proposals of mimetic realism from the conventional theatre to diverse fractures of codes. The characteristics of his theatre have already been carefully studied: to develop this work of visual poetization of the image and of scenic collage, with its displacements and citations that put the theatre in intertextual relationship with other artistic registers.
>
> It seems to me that in this critique of representation the mirrors operate throughout this game of deconstructed cuts, multiplications, and dislocations of the image. They reinforce the critical dimension, self-reflexive, of the theatrical language Griffero insists upon ...
>
> The game of mirrors and its problematic of the reflected image makes the image appear and disappear in a proliferation of replies and simulations that dissipate the real as a presence, that is to say, as a reference. This appearance/disappearance potentially enters into dialogue—at least, in my reading—with one of the symbolic dimensions of the theme of disappearance: to know the phantasmal character, spectral, of the disappeared's body; a body that continues floating in memory below the double regime: ambiguous, irresolute—of the living and the non-living, of presence and absence, of the known and what isn't verifiable, of the real and the intangible, of what can be felt and

the discorporated. Working scenically with this dimension of presence/absence, of appearance/disappearance of the body on the stage and of the stage of the body, the visual disposition of images in *Brunch* imaginatively connects with the problematic imaginary of the disappeared body, with the disappearance of the body and the memory of its disappearance …

I agree with the author and his insistence that only by creating new codes and perceptions (that is to say, moving rhetorical conventions beyond those established by cultural genres), will there be a means by which to let loose an imaginary that puts the vocabularies of the uniform and conformity in contradiction with those that the official culture seeks to accustom our gaze to through the passivity of the signs.

(Theatre conference paper, Universidad de Chile, 1999)

Finally, the theatre director Marcos Guzmán gives us another perspective on this production:

In the function of the text, the staging of *Brunch* reveals itself to us as a truly mortal trap that threatens and puts at risk all our sensibilities and our intellect. Because the beauty of the game of doubling and its shadows is capable of horrifying us to the infinite…

**PHOTOGRAPH 15** *Almuerzos de Mediodía o Brunch*.

Producing a true poetic dialogue between distinct languages, moving us away from simple and anecdotal explanations, whether they be of text or image. Thus, we are allowed to accede to moments of deep seduction. In a voyage without transitions from the overflowing images towards a species of tentative rest of the word … Griffero allows with absolute creative liberty that one works with more than his text, with the fissures that text provokes, because he evidently understands that more important than the words, are the voids that provoke those words to cross the space and the actors. *Brunch* gives us the marvelous possibility of past, present, and future in the same instant on the stage, reconstructing pieces of our history, working painfully not from *fiction* but from *our memory*.

(Marcos Guzmán, "*Almuerzos de mediodía, Brunch*," https://griffero.cl/almuerzo-de-mediodia-brunch/)

**PHOTOGRAPH 16** *Almuerzos de Mediodía o Brunch.*

## *Tus Deseos en Fragmentos*—2003

The space as a labyrinth of the mind

The motivation for this play is the construction of a mental space, a journey through the internal museum of our sensory emotions, a journey through the rooms of our memories and their personal experiences. The stage directions don't define its places and temporalities since they are already immersed in the interior of the text. The subtitle of the play is "conceptual irruptions" and signals to us the place where its spatiality is constructed, which is explicated in the play's stage directions:

> *Where to read from*
> *From inside the fragments of a brain. Actions are presented linearly on the page, but happen simultaneously on the stage.*
>
> *They occur where the situations interconnect read spatially, by means of the mechanisms of the visual narrative. (Objects, projections).*
>
> *These texts should be visualized for the stage from the perspective of an archeologist, behind the ideas (concepts) lie cities... Temples to disembowel*
>
> *Scenic installations*
> *These texts are written for multiple installations that form and disappear, producing the feeling of a mental labyrinth, where ideas, dreams, desires, intersect with a world of plastic and conceptual images, or points of reality that deliver a parallel perception to that of the verbal action described.*

The following critical reflections give us a sense of the spatial textual perception of the production:

> We are confronted by a cold stage structured in perpendicular axes. Windows, doors, and seats obey vertical and horizontal lines that violently cross each other. Crossing each other, they create several spaces inhabited by the actors, who place themselves in distinct depths of the proscenium,

taking possession of a specific place and then another, as if they were colonizing hostile territory. Thus, each situation pictured has its own physical space, that flowers by virtue of the action performed. The means—seats, walls, doors, and spatial subdivisions are quite well chosen. The unfolding of the structure generates surprise with neon lights and sharp angles that at first glance threatens to be extremely simple and sensational. That same lighting, and the preferential use of metal, gives the environment an appropriate coldness as surroundings for the laying bare of the desires of the twenty characters the six actors incarnate. Bearing witness to so much private conversation, and bared feelings, the deliriums and truths revealed between sex and caring have an impact. And the principal motive for what impresses us lies in that they are in their spontaneous enunciations, emulating the language of passion in a verisimultudinous manner. Fear of rejection and abandonment, one's own shame and that of others, cynicism and candor, honesty and lie, are all manifested in the characters, making them tender and lovable, as well as desirable.

(Romina de la Sotta, Radio Beethoven, 2003)

PHOTOGRAPH 17 *Tus Deseos en Fragmentos.*

The theatre researcher and essayist Gloría María Martínez digs into the conception, space/text of this play:

> To fragment, blow things up into multiple meanings seems to be more or less the constant in the contemporary theatre. Griffero's achievement lies in summoning this from the text. There seems to be a museum of memories-desires, and we never know if the museum is on the stage or if we are the spectators. This is not gratuitous. There is fluctuation between "to see and to be seen" that constitutes, evidently, a dramaturgical choice: if the choice were that we are shown to the spectators, this "showing" isn't produced by searching through illusions of reality, but by a constant disarticulation of the dramatic situations and of the "characters" inserted into them. The scenery is conceived in that same sense: Where does something happen? Here in the space of the stage convention or there where "you" are sitting?
>
> Minimal scenery: hospital—museum—Europe—boat—one's own room… In a short time it's all the same. Time isn't important either: yesterday, before yesterday, years ago, present, future…

PHOTOGRAPH 18 *Tus Deseos en Fragmentos.*

The only concrete and convoked space is that which travels through the spectator's body. Time is like the characters, that in which you are, and another previous one, and it is and isn't, like everything in this staging. The direction of the actors reflects this same fragmentation/disintegration. And it isn't a matter (as is more or less usual) of showing disconnected fragmented scenes for the spectator to associate with, intervene with their "look" to afterwards or during to give it meaning, through analogies and associations and construct the dramaturgy (in the sense of working with the actions) of the show. There is a greater finesse here, that isn't Stanislavkian in segments, or Brechtian, Meyerholdian, or Grotowskian ... although all these techniques are there, but not exhibited, not invisible but aesthetically and ideologically transubstantiated by a director ... Finally, what is happening, is it happening or happening to you? Are these the character's desires? The author's? Yours as spectator, but presented as if they were yours "in fragments"?

Nothing is as it seems: the space is whichever space, or the spaces your mind invokes, perhaps that is the space.

(Theatre conference paper, Universidad de Chile, 1999)

PHOTOGRAPH 19 *Tus Deseos en Fragmentos.*

# Fin de Eclipse—2007

## The space as support for the stories of our fictions

*A torn painted curtain, behind the tear a nude body.*
*She is drawing a costume on his body.*
(Stage directions from the play)

*Fin de Eclipse* is structured by means of a collection of scenic installations that arise from the story and constitute a labyrinth of fictions where we try to represent diverse scenic conventions from theatre history.

The idea is a labyrinth structured without a center, changes in narrative planes and characters that transmute and interlace on the basis of death and dream from the previous scene.

A sum total of awakenings, fictions, reveries that are reiterated, establishing the changes in planes, and the continuity of the characters in different temporalities.

This is added to power's discomfort in awakening our recognition that all discourses are fictions about reality designed to maintain a necessary order. But these vanish, contradict themselves, and reinstate themselves, only with the final goal of giving sustenance to certain thoughts about existence. We shouldn't believe that the perception of "truth" can be found in theatricality, but that it can be put in doubt by means of it, its constant installation.

*Fin de Eclipse* is perhaps a play about how to construct fictions, a text about creation. There is a fable where the theatre dreams about itself, and where in its interior death doesn't exist, since it is inserted in a fiction. This allows stories to begin again and return to existence and, thus, in a labyrinthine spiral, are only limited by the external temporality of the theatrical fact.

In this way, a structure emerges that allows it to contain multiple fictions, and these can disturb things at the same time from its interior, as if trying to break the dogmas of reality, or the theatre, that carry us to a place when destiny and parallel dimensions don't coordinate with them. Where each apparent end is not only a new beginning, but also a change, and where endings can also be replaced. The text aids scenic memory, the central question for the assimilation of its narrative.

*Fin de Eclipse* brings us from the Conquest, to the Romanticism of 1880, to the contemporary world, to people who love each other and their alter egos, from the war in Iraq to awakening on Cuban beaches, to remembering executions following a coup d'etat, to the moments in which a group of revolutionaries reunite, to the allegory of a happy theatre, to the metaphysics of looking at the universe as the only place in which we can evade ourselves.

It is from this multiplicity of places that one can dream about what happens, where what is spoken about is performed, or the stage comments on an event and contradicts what has been performed. There is clear evidence that the play speaks about and from the theatre and makes an apology for what has come before. What is unclear is finally whether talking from the theatre is necessarily to talk about creation or about reality.

Without doubt, it also points to how forms of theatricality try to contain and reinterpret our states of being and existence and the (in)capacity of one to be able to achieve the other. If we were to perform archeology on the text, and discover its transversal lines, there is undoubtedly love—romantic or impossible. Love united with death. Love and passion. And when I speak of love I speak of a place where sex doesn't exist, where it is centered more on the necessity of reencountering the other and giving them a meaning for life, a necessity for the theatre and for existence. Finally, *Fin de Eclipse* might be able to be the impossibility of creating a fiction.

The words of Coca Duarte, in the program for the play, amplify a view of the work and the production for us:

> Ramón Griffero's return to Chile at the beginning of the 1980s accelerated the theatrical renovation of our country. His theatrical proposal is based on what has been baptized as the dramaturgy of space.
>
> The dramaturgy of space supposes the assumption of the visual and spatial character of the theatre. Two fundamental principles can be enunciated. First, theatrical images can be composed using the same principles applied to painting in its rectangle since the Renaissance, incorporating the impact that using this convention in film has had upon the spectator. Thus, Griffero's theatre uses the tension of diagonals, variable depths of field, proportional division of the space, visual weight, cinematographic framing. Second, the theatre can (and should) abandon continuous

PHOTOGRAPH 20 *Fin de Eclipse.*

structuring based on being chained to words to investigate the work of production. In film, the work of production is to order discontinuous film slices to create meaning by juxtaposition. The work of cutting and reordering gives Griffero's theatre great flexibility and the capacity to awaken surprising associations.

One mustn't suppose that Ramón Griffero's theatre is the rigid application of these principles. Above all it is a creative exploration of the significance of space.

With the end of the dictatorship a stage of his creation also came to an end. After years of silence, Griffero went from exploring space as a place of collective encounter to the exploration of subjective space. Although his aesthetic proposal has developed and renovated, it continues faithful to the principle that the theatre is, above all, a visual construction and not "literature" performed.

It is possible to understand *Fin de Eclipse* as a deep reflection on the role of the theatre as a platform for investigating History. This time, Griffero chooses to stage the problematics of creating a text, putting his own writing practice and the role of the author as the creator of a fiction into question. Although he recognizes

PHOTOGRAPH 21 *Fin de Eclipse.*

History as mother and muse, he shows its cruelty and lack of consideration in the text: The fall of the Acropolis produces more horror in me than a building full of immigrants tumbling down.

At the same time, creating an analogy between History and the creation of the character He, recognizes the fictive quality of this physique. History has also been created by those who have told it.

Finally, Griffero rescues the author's role with the image of the eclipse. If we take the words of "That One": "if the sun doesn't want to light the earth, it is because it doesn't want to see what is happening, this is produced when violent facts cloud the face of the earth. But it is possible to revenge oneself with "others who eclipse my body, yours, hers". "Writing phrases to be lived by others, on the remains of stages that are left in clandestine forgetting, for the three who listen, dress themselves again with these phrases, whisper them between dark walls, like our secrets. The rest continue believing in what they must believe, phrases that will never succeed in clothing their souls.

*Fin de Eclipse* is, certainly, a good literary work. But what is presented in this theatre isn't that but something else, a density of signs and sensations to use Roland Barthes' famous formula. That is to say, a spectacle that is of the theatre, in which the space plays a fundamental role. This space opens and changes, like a cross between a Russian doll and a Rubik's cube. This changeable space full of evocations allows a word that isn't the one we use every day. The language of *Fin de Eclipse* is the language of thought.

In the productions I have cited a multidimensional plot construction is being inscribed where parallel times—from yesterday or imagined—mental, unconscious, lived times all commingle.

Where the fable is directed more towards our human condition on a planet where the metaphysical and the social are fused together. Scenic actions that try to demystify the existing fiction. To investigate what in our species creates armies and generates institutional psychopaths and is incapable of building the social desires it proposes, at the same time that it bathes us with deep sentiments of community and affection.

If the future defines itself in terms of yesterday, as the present constantly fades away, our artistic task today must reconfigure itself where the politics of art and autonomy, as well as social creation, are its motors as it confronts the inequities of neoliberalism and the pandemic.

Zoom theatre-art, a practical application that has installed itself due to social solitude and the current urgency, has been obliged to incorporate audiovisual narratives into plays and actions presented through this virtual rectangular format. One that interlaces with social networks constructing a new network of theatres, supplanting for an instant the empty theatres that await us in this new exterior.

The scenic art of tomorrow will have the challenge of depicting the emerging perceptions of this age's spirit, of reciting a patrimony, of adding letters to the scenic alphabet, of establishing a substantial break from the pre-pandemic creative gestures. The theatre is never in crisis, nor loses its sense of existence, it is only those of us who do this work who have to navigate the different energies that now shape our lives.

*I've found the crack of happiness ... I should drown myself in the canals today, this wandering, stop revenging myself on history, I'll never succeed, and breathe so alone, breathe as long* as the air exists. I've discovered love for the air, it's what has allowed me to sigh, drown myself and emerge from this ocean. We are only fish beneath the air, and I won't let anyone throw their nets over us, we will survive. I have discovered the world and the world is ours.

(*La Iguana de Alessandra*)

PHOTOGRAPH 22 *Fin de Eclipse.*

PHOTOGRAPH 23  *Fin de Eclipse.*

**PHOTOGRAPH 24** Dramaturgy of Space exercise.

# EPILOGUE

## The Labyrinth of Creation

The word doesn't try to be anything more than an illuminating agent of unreachable themes.

The word is only a summary, marks the boundaries of a present without being able to contain that which we should enunciate, given that its temporality fails to cover the parallelism or simultaneity of the mental planes that constitute the idea.

The symbiosis of the word with a poetics of space, elaborating from that complicity a dramaturgy of space, permits it to overflow its own narrative capacities.

We could say that language is our most tyrannous censor and functions as the major conciliatory element of our pulsations and desires. From there comes the constant rebirth of stories searching for ways to re-elaborate their concepts, name the situations and conflicts of a species that believes that through the word and dialogue it will succeed in taming the instincts of its deformed renegade essence, but only arrives at an elaboration of its eternal self-criticism.

A constant religion for the expiation of the sins of our own making and the proposition of fiction as an earthly paradise. But from whichever place it is spoken or told, whichever place annuls ideals that, once more, are only syllables.

It seems that we've arrived at one of those many borders, at the limits of not believing in or not being able to contain language, and, therefore, the discourses it elaborates.

It is the sensation of that abyss, the necessity of reconstructing thoughts and of giving other meanings to our existence, the motor of the labyrinth of creation.